THE

OF THE

THE WAITING MONTHS ON THE HILLTOP FROM THE ENTRANCE OF THE STARS AND STRIPES TO THE SECOND VICTORY ON THE MARNE

BY

MILDRED ALDRICH

AUTHOR OF "A HILLTOP ON THE MARNE," "TOLD IN A FRENCH GARDEN, AUGUST, 1914," "ON THE EDGE OF THE WAR ZONE"

BOSTON

SMALL, MAYNARD AND COMPANY

PUBLISHERS

This scarce antiquarian book is included in our special *Legacy Reprint Series*. In the interest of creating a more extensive selection of rare historical book reprints, we have chosen to reproduce this title even though it may possibly have occasional imperfections such as missing and blurred pages, missing text, poor pictures, markings, dark backgrounds and other reproduction issues beyond our control. Because this work is culturally important, we have made it available as a part of our commitment to protecting, preserving and promoting the world's literature. Thank you for your understanding.

THE PEAK OF THE LOAD

THE PEAK OF THE LOAD

I

Dear Old Girl: *April 20, 1917*

I HAVE had a rather busy two weeks, during which, for many reasons, I have not felt in the spirit to sit down and write you the long letter I know you expect in response to your great epistolary cry of triumph after the Declaration of War.

Personally, after the uplift the decision gave me, came a total collapse and I had some pretty black days. I had to fight against the fear that we were too late, and the conviction that, if we were really to do our part at the front, the war was still to last not one year, but years. An army cannot be created in a day, and the best will in the world, and all the pluck I know our lads to have, will not make them, inside of at least a year, into a fighting army fit to stand against the military science of Germany, and do anything more serviceable than die like heroes.

Besides, no matter from what point of view one looks at the case, it does make a difference to think that *our* boys are coming over here to go into this holocaust.

You must know that, even among officers in the army, who welcome with enthusiasm the entrance of the States into the ranks of the Allies, there are plenty who are still optimistic about the war's duration, and who smile, and say: "Don't fret. Your boys will march in the triumphal procession. The generous aid the States have given us earns them that right, but they cannot get ready to fire their guns in time to do much at the front."

I hope you'll take it in the right spirit when I say that I don't want it to end like that, and I am sure it won't. Personally I think the end is a long way off, and I can't tell you how our boys are needed. Besides, put it at the fact that Fate is to take a proportionate toll from our army — the other nations will have had nearly four years, if not quite four, before our losses begin.

Our men are going to leave their women and children in safety, in a land that can never know the horrors of invasion. I don't want to dwell on that idea, but it is a comfort all the same.

You say in your last that our boys are coming across the ocean "to die in a foreign land." Yes, I know. But they are coming to a country where they are already loved. Wonderful preparations are going to be made to care for them, and I do believe the United States, as a government and as a people, is going to make the great sacrifice

— economic, material and spiritual — which the situation demands of her in a manner which will make us all proud of her as a nation and will set a seal of nobility on the future of the race, and place our sort of democracy in the front ranks forever.

More than that, I believe that the States will come out of it more united than they have ever been, and, I hope, with the many elements, resulting from our long wide-opened door of immigration, welded into a people.

You and I, who love our country, in spite of, not because of, her faults, can surely at this stage of the game agree that the lessons we are going to learn are needed, and that out of the sorrow we *know* is before us may come results that could *never* have been achieved otherwise.

I — who have been living so long in the midst of it, and have seen with what undying gaiety youth meets even these conditions — smile even through the certainty of later tears when I think of some aspects of the situation. Just reflect, for example, on the thousands of our boys who never dreamed of "coming to Europe," who don't even know its geography or its history, who never bothered about architecture or archæology, who are going to make the voyage across the big pond. They are going to see foreign parts, hear foreign tongues, rub elbows with races they never saw or thought of seeing before. They are going to have hard times but crowds facing hard times together seem to get some fun out of it. They are going to be hardened into fine physical form by exercise. They are going to learn discipline which, if the youth of any country ever needed, ours does, and they are going to learn the meaning of obedience, which the youth of America, accustomed to domineer over its elders, will be the better for learning.

You see I always look for the compensations, and, as I have told you before, if one looks hard enough, they are to be found.

In my mental vision always hangs the idea, which so many are fearful to face — death is the common fate of us all.

However, I never sit up straight at a thought so ordinary, with such calm philosophy, that a little imp does not, with a malicious gesture, sweep the mists out of my eyes, and make me realize that, from Macaulay — with his:

> "To every man upon this earth
> Death cometh soon or late,
> And how can man die better
> Than facing fearful odds
> For the ashes of his fathers
> And the temples of his gods?"

To the priest in his pulpit, the orator in his tribune — and me sitting before my typewriter — words are easy. Yet even when I smile, I know that you and I, and oh! how many million others, would rather be out there "somewhere in France" than sitting quietly, inactively, at home, looking at the thick curtain which the necessary censor hangs before us, and waiting in patient suspense. The helpless looker-on in any struggle suffers more than those who are absorbed in its action. Is n't it a mercy that we believe this, whether it be wholly true or not? Also, though Macaulay sounds grandiloquent, the idea is as true to-day as it was in the days of old Rome of which he wrote, for our boys are coming over *not* to fight for France, but to fight for Liberty, which is the very altar of our national existence, and for the same ideas for which our ancestors — the founders of the original Union, now ashes, — laid down their lives.

I don't mean this to be a sad letter. I am not exactly sad. My feeling is too big a one for that. But I think we are all of us learning to-day to think of death more calmly, more continually, and more philosophically, than we have ever done. We are getting above the sentiment that it is a subject to be avoided, and arriving, quite naturally, at a mood which used only to be common to those who had reached an age at which it was natural and logical to feel that it might be encountered at any moment. I think it a great advance anyway. But we will talk more about that another time.

Things are pretty quiet here now.

After the sunny weather which came in to celebrate the entrance of the Stars and Stripes came some pretty cold days, and on one of them, when I was shivering over a tiny fire made of green twigs, came the news that the 118th had been badly cut up behind Soissons in the last advance, and that of all the little group who had stood about me in the library that sunny Sunday morning, but *one* was left.

I just put my cap on and went out to walk.

I kept telling myself that "it was all right," as I tramped along the road—that in half a century all of us in and about this great struggle, would be safely *au delà,* and that though men die, and women, too, the idea for which they die to-day is immortal. It looks easy on paper, but—*my word!*—it is *not.* I have to fight for it. You will soon have to, on your side of the water.

Activity is the only help. I came back and worked like a dog—my dog does not work at all—tidying up all the stuff left over by the *cantonnements,* making heaps of straw and other débris on the side of the road and trying to burn it.

I had given it some weeks to dry, but it had not done its part very well. The result is that it is not all burned yet. I light it half a dozen times a day, and it smoulders. Some time I expect it will all be burned, and then we 'll spread it over the garden. So, instead of putting any more words on paper, I ought to go out to rake that brush fire up again.

Incidentally I 'll look off at the hill and down the valley. All the fruit trees are in flower. Down the hill towards Condé there are lovely pink clouds which mark the peach trees, and across the Morin, to the south, the plum trees are like dainty white mists. The alleys in the garden at Père's look like a millinery show, all wreaths of apple blossoms strung on the trellises that border the paths, and the magnolia parasol, which marks, with its spreading shape, the middle of the path, and under which Amélie sits in summer to darn my stockings, is already putting on its young green cover. I am going to send you a photograph of that garden path one day.

Of course we don't talk or think of anything here but the German retreat—Hindenburg's famous strategic retreat. No one denies that the whole thing has been a great lesson in military science, were it not for its accompaniment by acts so unmilitary as to put another blot on the very word "German."

Every one has a different way of regarding the fact that—possibly to avoid or outwit the threatened Allied spring offensive — Hindenburg felt it prudent to establish a new and stronger line of defence thirty kilometers in the rear of the line he had been holding so long, — a line to-day known as the Siegfried line. Whether or not we were outwitted history will tell us some day in the future — I suppose. The fact from which there is no getting away is that, although this move was rumoured even among civilians as long ago as July of last year, he succeeded in doing it, and that in spite of the fact that the Allied pursuit was prompt and more or less harassed his rear, and perhaps pushed him further and more rapidly than he at first intended.

Soldiers do not deny the cleverness of the move, but the acts of no military import which accompanied the retreat fill us with horror. To destroy roads and bridges, to cut down forests and raze houses that could have served as shelters or military posts, well, any army would do that. But to poison wells, to uproot orchards, to carry off young girls — these are acts of war that are — to say the least — unmilitary. It is no use talking about it. But what a ruined northeast France it is! Yet, in spite of that, almost the day after the retreat began the poor refugees who had left in August, 1914, began to hurry back, ready to reconstruct their devastated homes. It is a wonderful spirit, and thank God for it! It is to be the saving of France.

I wonder if mere words on paper can make any one realize exactly what has happened. I am sure that, horror-stricken as we have been by some of the details, we have no full sense of it, and how can you, merely reading it in letters of black and white in a newspaper, realize what it is hard for us to take in when it is told us by men who looked on it? Imagine 264 villages wiped off the map: towns like Chauny, a big industrial centre where there were bleach fields and chemical works, razed: 255 churches and 38,000 houses reduced to mere heaps of rubbish. Can you take it in? I confess that it is hard for me.

I saw an officer who was in the pursuit who told me that the Boches left groups of women who had been outraged shut up in cellars in the ruined towns and villages, and carried off all the girls in their late 'teens. What a record for "Kultur"! Does it not wipe the word out of all decent vocabularies and inscribe it among those forbidden and hidden away in pornographic dictionaries?

The demoniac ingenuity of the destruction really surpasses all the demonstrations of German efficiency which this war has yet brought to notice. You have probably read that they sawed down all the orchards and did their utmost to render the fertile soil for a long time unproductive. But that was rather a large order, I am afraid. At any rate they made inanimate objects their infernal aid. They left hidden mines to explode. They left large trees standing, along where roads had once been, sawed almost through, so that the first strong wind would send them crashing on engineers at work repairing the roads or convoys passing in pursuit. My word! but these Germans give the traditional Old Nick all the trumps in the pack and beat him still in devilishness.

You remember Coucy-le-Château, that marvellous ruin, which Violet-le-Duc considered the finest specimen in Europe of medieval military architecture, and which after two hundred and fifty-six years of existence was dismantled by Mazarin in 1652, and has since then been a public monument — a wonderful ruin? I am sure you have climbed over it, every one has, and sat in the shade and looked off at the view. I had a letter the other day from a cavalry officer who is now stationed there, in which he said, "You thought it a ruin when you saw it. You should see it now. The brutes!"

In the meantime, the English are still outside St. Quentin, to the very outskirts of which the French cavalry pushed in March. That has always been a fatal spot to the French. It is rather ironical to remember that it was near St. Quentin — which was part of the dower of Mary, Queen of Scots, — that the French were defeated three hundred and fifty years ago by the allied English, German and Flemish armies, and that there, in January, 1871, the French Armée du Nord was beaten by General Goeben of the Prussian forces. I shall feel more easy in my mind once the English are in the town, although we hear that it is largely destroyed — another big factory town — a sort of French Lowell or Lawrence — gone.

In your last letter you reproach me because I say "nothing about Russia." Yes, I know — Russia is our "great delusion." What can one say? I have never known much about Russia. I used to *think* I did. Most of the Russians I knew were revolutionary men who were political exiles here. But I have been no greater fool about it than most of the governments of this world. What can I say except that I suppose they are going to fail us — and then what? Well, one thing is certain, the curtain is getting torn and we are likely to know more about the Russians than we have ever known — to our cost. You need not bother to twit me that I used to say the "Russians were a great people." Of course I did, and I say it still. They may not prove it until I have gone on, but that is not important.

You may have the laugh on me. But is it worth while? You have it on a lot of big people. Let that content you. Besides, the only thing you ever had against the Russians was that they were "queer," and that their language was "hard to learn." And then you did not like the paintings they exhibited at the Salon. My reasons for liking them were better than yours for disliking them. I suppose that I shall find excuses for them if the very worst that can happen comes to pass. So don't think you can take any rise out of me on that subject. There are a great many other things that I think about which I do not write to you. To begin with, the censor would work on my letters with his ink brush, and you would be none the wiser, and I would have bothered myself in vain.

II

May 1, 1917

I HAD hardly mailed my last letter to you when things got very exciting here again.

Early in the morning of April 24—that was Tuesday of last week—we heard that the cavalry was trotting into the valley again, and that we were to have the 32nd Dragoons quartered on us.

Naturally, the first thing I said was, "What a pity it isn't the 23rd," which was so long with us in the winter that we felt it was really *our* regiment. When the 32nd began to ride in we learned that the 23rd was not far off—only five miles down the valley at La Chapelle, just opposite Crécy-en-Brie.

Well, I could not complain, for I had another charming young officer in the house—another St. Cyr man, a lieutenant with a "*de*" to his name—a man a little over thirty, and very *chic*.

On Wednesday—that was the 25th—I was sitting in the library trying to work, when I heard an unusual movement in the road, and looked out to see a group of five officers of the 23rd, followed by a couple of orderlies, dismounting at the gate — coming to make an afternoon call — all booted and spurred and fresh-gloved and elegant, as if there were no such thing as war, though they were burned and bronzed by the campaign from which they had but just retired.

It was good to see them again, especially the Aspirant, and though I would have liked to hear all the details of the famous "strategic retreat," I got only a few, as of course you know it is forbidden the soldiers to talk to civilians, and a good thing, too.

However, I did hear a few interesting things, one of the most striking being that when the French cavalry dashed through Noyon, the poor French people did not recognize them. The population in the invaded district was waiting for the famous *pantalon rouge*. They did not even know that their army had changed its uniform, and when they saw the blue-grey cavalry coming they thought it was still the enemy and ran to hide again.

They told me that the joy of these poor people who had been two years and a half under the German heel, when they finally realized that it was their own army which had arrived, was pathetic.

Hardly had the group of officers taken leave, and ridden up the hill, when Lieutenant de G—— came in to sit down for a little chat about home and children. I can't tell you how these men like to talk about home. In the course of the conversation I made arrangements with him to have some of his horses and men help in the fields the next morning, for the work here is terribly behind.

When he went down the hill to dinner I rushed to tell Amélie, and to have everything ready for next morning, and you can imagine my disappointment, when, at nine, Lieutenant de G—— came in, quite disconsolate, to tell me that orders had arrived to sound "Boots and Saddles" at half past six the next morning.

I ought not to have been surprised for the officers of the 23rd had told me that it was not a long stay—only an *étape*.

The next morning—that was last Thursday—was a beautiful day. I was up early. I met Lieutenant de G—— on the stairs, where he bowed over my hand, and made me such a pretty, graceful speech of thanks for my hospitality—you can count on any French soldier, from an officer down to the ranks, doing that.

I had hardly got out into the garden after he left, when a detachment of the 23rd pulled up at the gate, and the *sous-officier* in command, saluted, as he said: "Aspirant B——'s compliments. The 23rd is cantonning at Mareuil to-night. I am going ahead to arrange the *cantonnement*. If it is possible the Aspirant counts on calling on you this afternoon to make his adieux. We march again to-morrow," and with another salute the little troop galloped down the hill.

The 23rd rode away at half past seven, and they passed the 6th Dragoons riding in, to take their places.

The little body of cavalry that came up our hill was in command of a *maréchal des logis* — a handsome, tall, slender lad of not over twenty, — who explained that it was only a twenty-four-hour rest for men and horses. They carried no kitchens at all, — no revictualment of any sort. Each man had two days' rations in his *sac,* and the horses carried their feed-bags and oats.

It was a new kind of *cantonnement* for me, and the most picturesque I had ever seen.

When everything had been arranged the *maréchal des logis* came to the door and asked if I could conveniently put him up.

I led him to his room, and you would have laughed if you could have seen his expression when I showed him the big freshly made-up bed.

"Am I going to sleep in that?" he exclaimed, and then we both laughed as if it were a real joke. You see we need so little excuse to laugh these days.

The weather was beautiful.

The boys sat or lay all along the roadside

in the sun, and the horses, relieved of all equipment, and well brushed, were tethered to the banks and in the courts, wherever there was a blade of grass — in fact they were "turned out to grass" for the first time since last fall, — while the soldiers ate and smoked and slept beside them, or rolled, frolicking like youngsters full of springtime spirit. It was the most unmartial, bucolic sight imaginable.

There was not much pasturage for the horses, and I looked at my lawn, and at what Louise calls the "*prairie*" under the fruit trees, and I went out in the road and ceremoniously invited as many of the best-behaved horses as could feed there to come in to lunch.

The *maréchal des logis* was writing letters in the salon when I led my little cavalcade along the terrace — they had selected the most obedient horses who did not even need halters — and he came out to say that it was a pity to trample my lawn — as if I cared for that!

You, who so adore horses, would have loved to see them. There was plenty of good feed. There was sunshine and shade, and they nibbled and snorted, while the soldiers who had charge of them rolled on the grass and smoked. I did wish I could have got a snapshot for you, but no one had a camera.

As it was Thursday Louise was working in the garden—Thursday is her day. Suddenly she shaded her eyes and looked down towards the Marne, and called out to me that Aspirant B—— was coming. Sure enough, there he was, coming on foot across the fields as if he had seven-league boots, and waving his cap. Mareuil, where the 23rd had gone, is only two miles away.

He arrived hot and breathless, to explain that, while he was not really out of bounds, still he had not asked permission and so had come on foot, and dared not stay long, but that he could not bear to leave the *Seine et Marne* without coming to say good-bye, as orders might come at any moment to advance, and no one had the faintest idea what their destination would be.

I had half a moment's foolish hesitation, as I remembered that the *maréchal des logis* was in the salon. I did not know what the military etiquette was, or how officers like to meet unceremoniously. So I said: "Shall we sit out here, or will you come into the salon? The *maréchal des logis* of the 6th is there."

"Oh, let's join him, of course," replied the Aspirant.

As I led the way I wondered how I was going to introduce them. I did not know the *maréchal's* name. But I need not have fretted.

I opened the door. The *maréchal* sprang

erect. The two youngsters both so tall, so slender and straight — saluted, flung their names at each other, thrust out their hands and gripped. Then they smiled, sat down, crossed their long legs, and fell to. It was like a drill — so exactly in unison — and so young and charming, that I just leaned back in my chair and listened and thought a lot.

Don't you know how there used to be a tradition about "little Frenchmen"? I vow I don't know where they all are now. I thought of it Wednesday when the group of officers stood about in my salon — their heads almost to the rafters — and I thought of it again to-day as I saw these two twenty-year olds — both nearly six feet, if not quite.

When the brief visit was over the lads parted like friends.

As the Aspirant was saying good-bye on the lawn, and laughing at the idea of my having "the horses in to tea," as he called it, although I called it "spending the day," he directed my attention to the road across the field by which he had arrived, and I looked down.

"Hulloa!" he exclaimed. "Here comes the 23rd racing to visit its pet *cantonnement* at Huiry. You know, Madame, they never have been so happy anywhere else as they were in what they call '*ce joli petit pays de Huiry.*'"

Sure enough, there came Hamelin and

Vincent, who had lodged at Amélie's, and Basset and all the rest who had lived about us in December and January.

So you see we had rather an exciting day.

The result was that I was very tired, and I slept very soundly.

As a rule when troops are here I always hear all the night movement. Whenever any officer in the house received a night message, in spite of all their precautions, I invariably heard the cyclist arrive. But that night I heard nothing. I waked at six. I opened my shutters. The sun was shining brightly. The morning was clear and warm. I looked out, wondering at the silence. I expected to see the horses being groomed all along the road. To my surprise all the stable doors were wide open — no one in sight, — no horses, no soldiers anywhere.

When Amélie appeared she said the order had come at midnight. They had marched at three — and I had not heard a sound. Am I not getting used to a military life?

But I must give you some evidence that the race famed for its politeness has not lost any of the quality in the war, and all its hurry.

Although Lieutenant de G——, who left Thursday morning, had formally thanked me for my hospitality, within twenty-four hours I received the following note from him.

Madame:

I must again express to you all my gratitude for the charming welcome you extended to me under your roof. Our roving life did not allow us to stay long at Huiry, but, thanks to you, we shall always cherish a charming recollection of our too short visit.

And, twenty-four hours after the 6th rode away in the night, I received the following letter from the young *maréchal des logis.* It seems to me such a pretty letter for a lad of twenty that you deserve to see it.

With the Army, April 28, 1917

Madame:

I hope you will have the kindness to excuse me if, before my departure this morning, I did not have the opportunity of thanking you for the charming welcome you extended to me in your pretty home. It was late when I came in last night, and it was still dark when we took leave of your dear little village this morning, and I was therefore unable to see you, to my deep regret, and to express to you in person all the gratitude I felt, and my deep joy to find that the sympathy which the Americans, our new allies, express for us, is no vain word. Your kindness to us all was the best of evidence, and I beg you to believe, Madame, that the sentiment is reciprocated.

All my men, as well as my two comrades and I, were deeply touched by the welcome extended to us in your village, and especially by you in person, and we should have been only too happy had we been able to stay with you longer. We are much less comfortable to-night than we were last night, but a soldier is forced to consider himself comfortable anywhere. All the same he is more than happy, now and then, to find himself among kind people who offer him the comforts of home of which he has been deprived for nearly three years. Even our horses are less gay than they were yesterday. This afternoon they had no green lawn to nibble.

I beg you, dear Madame, etc.

Maréchal des logis G——.

The politeness of these French boys and their aptness in writing letters promptly is remarkable. It is a national characteristic. It is a great contrast to the American *sans gêne* manner, which surprises French people. For example, all the French soldiers nursed in our little ambulance write immediately they get back to the Directrice, the Sisters, and their special nurse to reiterate the thanks they have so profusely expressed before leaving, and anyone to whom I have shown the smallest courtesy while there writes to me. The little hospital has never sheltered but one American. When he returned to his post every one gave him an address, and every one expected a postcard from him, at least. Of course he could not write French, but he could send a picture postcard with his name, and a line which he knew I would render into French. No word ever came back. Dear Sœur Jules is sure he is dead. I never see her but she asks: "Have you had news from ——?" And when I say, "No," she shakes her head sadly, and exclaims, "Poor lad! Of course he has been killed. Poor nice boy! We were so attached to him." I let it go at that. It is so hard to explain that it is very American.

Lovely day—so good after the terrible winter.

I am already planting peas and beans and potatoes. But the flower garden will not be very pretty this year, I lost so many rose bushes in the awful long spell of January and February cold. But what of that? Potatoes are the only *chic* thing this year. They are planted everywhere—on the lawn at the château, in the front gardens, under the fruit trees. I was tempted to plant them on my lawn, only that would have been pretentious, as Père had more land than we needed, and it would have cost more to turn up my lawn than the mere patriotic look of the thing was worth.

III

May 18, 1917

JUST the loveliest day you can imagine. When I went into the garden early this morning I did wish you were here. A soft puffy breeze was blowing, and a thin haze veiled the sun. There was only one word for it—divine. I never see the country looking as it did at that moment that I do not long to own a big camera and become an expert with it. It would only be in that way one could ever get a proper picture of it. It is so wilfully changeable that to do it justice—to catch it at its best—the camera would have to be on the spot—ever ready.

We have had a week of really hot weather. It has been good for planting, and I 've planted carrots and turnips and beets and onions, tomatoes and cucumbers, and if this lasts, I am going to try golden bantam corn. What do you think of that for a farmer? Hush—Louise does the hard work, and I boss it. I sit in the field on a camp chair with the seeds in a basket, and a green umbrella over my head, and big gloves on my hands, while Louise grovels in the dirt and carries out my ideas. I get terribly tired, and very red in the face, but Louise, brown as a berry, comes out fresh as possible.

Well, anyway, I am going to have something to eat — in time — and that comforts me.

At noon to-day it clouded over, and a cold wind came up which drove me indoors. Though it is as cold here as outside, still I am out of the wind, and that is how it happens that, though I have nothing much to write about, I am going to try to make a letter. Everything in the world is still — but though we hear no sound of cannon, I have the thought of it always with me. It is more persistent than the poor.

I have been looking over some of your letters, and I find that you have often asked me questions about my beasties, and because I have almost always had other things to write about I have never got to telling you about anything in the beastie line, except cats — and you got that, you remember because you were nasty about my efforts to "wake up the States," which had been hardly less successful at that time than dear Lord Roberts' great "Wake Up, England!"

Well, since you want to hear about beasties, so be it.

Of course, you remember that in the old days I never had any beasties in the apartment, except birds. When I came out into the country to live I did not see any place either in my little house or in my new life for that huge cage and the twenty birds that lived in it, in Paris.

I had loved them in the Paris apartment. High up in the air, with that broad open space across the Montparnasse cemetery to fill the wide balcony with sunlight and warmth, they had seemed quite in the picture. But the idea of caged birds on this hilltop seemed to me silly. What happiness could a cage full of birds have when surrounded by singing birds in liberty? Also every one out here kept cats.

In Paris, high up above the street, the morning concerts had been the only gay thing in the sad and lonely house. I learned to love them. I loved giving them their bath in the morning, doing up their house for them, and preparing their meals. I loved seeing them flying about, dancing and singing, swinging and balancing, and eating.

I loved believing they were happy. But I could not imagine them happy out here, so they did not come with me. I gave them and their gilded palace to some one whom they had always known, and now and then I still go to see them.

So when I came out here I had no beasties.

The first one I had was a dog. He was a beautiful Airedale — a big dog with a dear chestnut-coloured head and legs and belly, and a nicely fitting, undulated, black jacket.

But, alas! I did not have him long, and it was altogether a sad experience.

When he arrived he was homesick.

Did you ever see a homesick dog? Or, what is worse, did you ever live with one? For days, before he learned to love me, he followed me about in a patient, resigned way which made me pretty sad. I had not had much experience in owning beasties, except birds. I had to get acquainted as well as he. It was hard on both of us. Besides, the house was all fresh and clean, and, as I was determined that he should feel that it was as much his home as mine, he was allowed everywhere, and brought in a lot of dirt, and my habit of having everything in apple-pie order—by the way, what kind of order is that?—got a shock.

But I grew used to all that, and reconciled to it, as he became attached to me, and, even in the little time he stayed, I got so that I did not mind when he leaped all over me, and wiped his muddy paws, and he could not walk out with me without embracing me every few minutes. I was so grateful to him for showing pleasure in my society that for a while I did not even try to break him of it. I ended by getting deeply attached to him, and he to me. I was so proud of him. I loved walking out with him, carrying his leash and whip, with a whistle in my sweater pocket. He was naturally obedient. He always walked close to my heels except when I told him to "go," and then he was off like a flash. But he never went out of sight. If he reached a turn, he stopped to look back and see if I were coming, and if I hid he dashed back and sniffed around until he found me. Of course this is all commonplace to people who have always had dogs of their own. But it was a new experience to me.

If he saw anyone coming towards me he retired quietly to my side—not as if afraid, but as if to assure himself that I was not going to be molested. For a few weeks that was all right. He seemed gentle and was as playful, once he was domiciled, as a small dog.

I had never had a watch-dog—didn't know anything about them. I had him for company. But one day Amélie was sweeping the terrace. Argus was lying in the sun. I was standing at the gate, which was closed. The postman came up the road and started to open the gate. Argus was there in one bound. He snarled, then growled deep down in his throat. The man did *not* come in.

Amélie laughed aloud. Instinctively I said, "No, no, Argus!" but Amélie simply screamed at me: "*Laissez donc*," and she patted him on the head. "At last," she said. "I was wondering if that dog was anything but beautiful. Pat his head," she commanded, "and tell him he is a good dog." I obeyed orders, and Argus wagged his tail, and strutted, and from that day he was the terror of the *commune*. He never passed anyone on the road without growling, and he barked at every one who passed the gate.

Personally I thought he carried his ardour too far, since he could not bear a stranger near. He barked when they arrived, and he kept it up. Every one was afraid of him, though I was always convinced that he was not a dangerous dog. He never attacked anyone. On the road he always came the instant he was called, and patiently allowed himself to be leashed.

I confess I never got at his psychology—he did not live long enough. As I say, he never attempted to attack anyone, though he did attack a big dog. He never attached himself to anyone outside of the household. I had heaps of theories about him. At times I thought there was a savage strain in him. At other times I imagined he was as afraid of people as they were of him. But I don't know.

When he was ill, and I sent for the veterinary, Argus was upstairs lying at my bedroom door when the doctor arrived. I called him. He came half-way down the stairs and stood barking. The doctor said: "As handsome an Airedale as I ever saw, but I would not touch him for a fortune."

"But, doctor," I said, "he's perfectly gentle."

"With you, perhaps. I can't touch him."

So I went upstairs with the dog, and he let me tie up his nose, and I held him while the doctor examined him.

Well—he died. Never mind about that. I don't like even now to remember it. I like to think of him as we used to walk out together, when he was the first comrade of my new life.

Oh, yes, I have another dog now, but he is just a dog to me. I like him well enough, and play with him, but my heart is not set on him as it was on my big dog of whom I was so proud.

This dog's name is Dick. He is a big black poodle and a perfect fool. He is what the French call "*pas méchant pour deux sous*," just a common or garden fool. He is a thoroughbred, but he has never been trained at all, and as he was nearly, if not quite, four years old when he came—with his character—training has been impossible. He was bought when a baby as a plaything for a child at Couilly. When the war broke out, his family went to Switzerland and left Dick a boarder at Amélie's. At Couilly he left a bad reputation. A child had hit him with a stick and hurt him, and Dick had sprung on her—the one naughty act of his life, but it was enough to give him a bad name — so he had to come up here to live.

No one knows everything about a dog except after long years of experience. Though he is the silliest, gentlest, most playful dog in the world, though he adores children, and the cats sleep all over him, I have to own that he has never forgotten the child at Couilly who struck him with the big stick, and the very sight of her to-day — after more than five years — brings out a quality of ugliness in him that he never shows at any other time. Apart from that one trait he is a comic, frolicsome dog, whose delight in life is to "go," and whose dream of happiness is to have anyone, no matter whom, throw stones for him.

He was boarding at Amélie's when I came here. While Argus lived he never came near the house. But after Argus had gone Amélie used to bring him down here with her, and I got used to seeing him about. Neither Amélie nor Abélard had been content that there was no dog here at night, and finally I consented to let Dick sleep in the kennel; he has been sleeping there ever since. The only protection he gives is to bark when anyone approaches the house, and that is really all that is necessary. When he barks furiously in the night — as every one knows his voice, — someone comes to be sure that I am all right.

When I say he barks at every one, that's not quite true. He *used* to bark at every one, but, for some reason, since we have had so many soldiers cantonned here, he never barks at a *poilu*. It is the only exception. He barks at the children, at the postman, at the neighbours he sees every day on the road, but he never barks in these days at a common soldier. Droll, that, I think! I have asked him to explain himself, but I am too stupid to understand.

Of course Mélie has a big dog — a black retriever — who, though he is already huge, is hardly more than a puppy. He came last winter, and I named him Marquis, and it was at once abbreviated into Kiki. Amélie brought him in her apron one night when he was about as big as a small cat, and showed him to Khaki and Didine. Khaki gave one look at him, and asked for the door. He shrugged his shoulders as he went out with very stiff legs and a line of bristling hair down his back, as much as to say "Another? Dear me!" But Didine went up to him as he lay on Mélie's knee, examined him, and deliberately cuffed him first on one side of his head, and then on the other, and hard cuffs, too. Marquis has grown up since 'hen, but he has no taste for cats.

Although Marquis is still only a puppy, he is already much bigger than Dick, and Dick is still just as much of a puppy — and will be to the end of his days — and it is lovely to see them play together — such races and boxing matches as they have! They don't always observe the rules of the Marquis of Queensbury to be sure, but they never get cross over their game. Marquis is just as good a sport as Dick, but though he is heavier he does not tire so easily, and often when Dick retires to his corner to get his breath back and lies with his tongue hanging out, Marquis goes and pulls him into the ring by his hind leg.

So there you have the dogs that run with me when I cross the fields. I have to keep them with me as all dogs must be leashed or muzzled. I carry muzzles and whip and whistle when I walk, and, as they are both obedient to the whistle, I can call them if I see anyone approaching, and get them on their leashes if I don't have time to muzzle them. Some time, if I get a chance, I'll ask them to send you their pictures.

Though I don't have birds, I have hens and chickens. I have four hens setting at Amélie's now. I don't want anything of that sort round here. So I have arranged an imitation of a *basse cour* and hen-house at Amélie's. You'd laugh if you could see it. I began it last summer. I sent Amélie to town to buy a dozen chickens — ten of them proved to be cocks, so we fed them to be eaten, and bought another dozen, with hardly better luck, except in the matter of winter food. I began the spring with a rooster and seven hens, and every one of those hens shall set if she wants to. Amélie pulls a long face, and says, "How are you going to feed them?" Well, if I can't, I can eat them, or give them to other people to eat.

Food is a very interesting question in these days. Besides, hens are about the only creatures I can contemplate eating with equanimity. They are amusing enough at feeding time, but they are ugly, selfish, unlovable birds, except when they have a brood of fluffy little ones about their feet, and then they are adorable.

The most amusing experience I have ever had was with goats,—and that one experience impressed on me the fact that I'd need several more years of training to become a real farmer, or a stock breeder,—perhaps even another incarnation.

When milk got short it was a serious dilemma, and the future looked even more serious. Milk is a very important item in my diet, and how we were to get through another winter short of milk was a question.

One day Amélie remarked that if we had a goat, that it would be some help, as she and Père liked goat's milk. So, one day, at Meaux, I told her I'd make her a present of a goat, if she could find one. I was amazed when she came back to the wagon carrying the cunningest little beastie in her arms you ever saw.

"Why, Mélie," I cried, "that won't give any milk!"

"Give it time," she replied. "It is such a pretty one."

So I named it Jeannette, and it came to live "at the farm."

It was as frisky as a kitten and we all made a plaything of it. It followed Mélie up and down from her house to mine, and when it got to know the way it came by itself to call. I was eternally catching it in my garden, standing on its hind legs, nibbling my rose bushes, and picking it up in my arms and carrying it home. But it was so fascinating on its stiff, wooden, peglike legs, and it side-stepped so gracefully when I was catching it, and danced on its hind feet, and butted at me sideways, that I could not get cross.

Sometimes I 'd hear a rustle in the hedge as I was reading in the shade, and, going out to the gate to see what was trying to get through, would find Jeannette standing on her hind legs, eating the old hedge with all her might. I did n't mind that. It did not hurt the hedge to be trimmed. But when she began to eat pansies, roses and geraniums, I drew the line, and protested. I drove her home one day, and began to ask myself if other goats had as much liberty as Jeannette, and decided that they did not and that, in fact, she was being badly brought up.

I looked over the fields and saw goats nibbling, each with a long rope attached to a stake.

So I went up to Amélie's to have a serious talk about the upbringing of her goat. I found Père — it was just afternoon — taking his nap in a big chair with Jeannette hugged in his arms as she lay on his knees.

I had to laugh. It was not a moment to argue.

The proper moment came a few days later.

It was early in the morning. I heard some one talking angrily in the road, and it only took a little listening to discover that Jeannette had been in a neighbour's garden and made a good meal of peas. The owner was angry, and I did not blame her. It was one thing for Jeannette to destroy my garden or Père's, but quite another matter when she went trespassing and laid us liable to a *procès*.

This time I stiffened my lips — I hate to argue with Mélie — and just went at the job. I emphatically stated that it was absurd to let a destructive animal like a goat roam at liberty, that goats were usually attached, and that there was no reason why Jeannette should not be. By the time I had done, Mélie was in tears.

"Poor Jeannette," she sobbed. "She loves her liberty, and I love mine, and can sympathize. Poor Jeannette, I know just how she feels."

Of course I had to say, "Sorry, Mélie, but we did not buy the goat for a plaything, and you know as well as I do that she cannot always run free, so one time is as good as another. There is plenty of place for her to eat. There is the little meadow out under the trees where she can be tied up. She will be near the house, and the grass there is full of all sorts of good things—dandelions, chicory, sanfoin, and there is the court here, and there is the little *enclos* at the top of the hill where we put the horse and donkey, and there is the grass land up the hill, and when once the *cassis* is gathered, she can be put there."

"Oh," replied Amélie, "there are places enough, if it must be done."

It was done, but it was too late to be done with comfort to anyone. Jeannette had been made a family pet. She was used to company. Wherever we put her she b-l-laated for hours at a time, unless one of us went and sat with her. I protested, but I used to catch Amélie taking her sewing to sit with Jeannette, and Père used to go and lie near her on the ground to take his noon nap—

and as long as she lived, she would never be cured of that longing for society, if not for liberty.

Well, the time came when Jeannette became a mother. It was about the quickest performance I ever knew of. It was a Thursday. Louise was working in the garden, as is usual on all Thursdays. She had gone to Père's to carry a wheelbarrow of grass — we had cut the lawn. I saw her returning without the wheelbarrow on a quick run, calling as she came, "Is there any hot water? Jeannette has got twins!"

I did not wait for Louise to get the hot water. I just sprinted — in my way — for the stable. There were the little long-legged things — walking, if you please, while Jeannette looked over her shoulder at them in wide-eyed surprise. Talk about cunning things! They beat all I had ever seen. They were both white. One had a thin black line down his spine to his cute little stub of a tail, and the other had a similar black line half as long. On the spot I named them — it's my way — Pierre and Paul.

For a few weeks those little goats were my every-day amusement. They were playful as kittens. We used to attach Jeannette up the road in an open field, and leave Pierre and Paul with her, but if I dared to heave in sight, both the little beasties rushed to meet me. Then Jeannette set up a yell, and

I had to catch them and take them back. Then I was as bad as Amélie, for I would sit in the shade and watch them. The field was up a bank, and they used to butt each other down, and dance and do side-steps until I used to call Amélie to come and look at them, and we would both sit, like a pair of geese, and laugh. I forgot as much as she ever had what the goat was bought for.

Pierre was a bit more venturesome than Paul. He was always the leader. The only queer thing was that they never varied their methods. For example, they would both come close to the door, and turning their heads sideways, look in. Then Pierre ventured in, and Paul followed. The dining-room was always darkened in the daytime to keep it cool, but the door was open. Pierre, followed by Paul, would come and look, and then, although there was no sill, bound in as though over a barrier, and, after a moment's hesitation, Paul did the same thing. There was hardly a day they did not come, and they never varied the antic, nor failed, when I went to catch them and put them in the stable at night, to side-step, bound sidewise on their hind legs, and butt at me with such a pretty turn of the head. But no one ever drew a picture or made an image of a goat in any other movement, so all goats must do it. Only these were the first with which I had ever been intimate.

Well, all country idyls end in tragedy.

Last Saturday—Saturday is market day at Meaux—after I had taken my coffee, which I got myself, as Amélie and Père had arranged to go to market early on account of the heat—I went up to the pasture to see why Jeannette was crying so. I found her still tied in the stable instead of in the pasture, as I had expected, and there was no Pierre and Paul.

I had a sort of sudden premonition. I went back, and sat in the garden until I heard the wagon coming. I gave one look at Mélie's red eyes. I did not have to ask. I knew that Pierre and Paul had gone to market.

Jeannette did not get over crying for days.

Well, as Père remarked, "She was bought to give us milk."

You see, next time I'll know how to bring up a goat. I can only be thankful I don't get attached to chickens. I've that much luck.

You can't call this a war letter, can you? The real absolute truth is that just now it is hard to believe there is any war, it is so calm and still here, and the nights are heavenly. I often sit out until midnight, and I have even fallen asleep with my head on my arms, simply hating to come indoors and leave all the beauty of the night. I wish often that I had one of those tents in which the Virginia boys slept on our common. I think it will be the next thing I present myself.

You can never realize the wonder of the nights here until you see them. It is not dark until after ten, — summer-time, of course. There is no sound except from the passing trains, and nothing breaks the line of the hills, except, now and then, the end of a searchlight from the other side, a thin line only, but it visualizes "war," reminding us that the watch is kept.

Of course we have all been bitterly disappointed again that the push does not go on. We don't understand, but we must have faith in those who do, — or we hope, do.

IV

June 15, 1917

I HAVE been so busy learning to be a farmer that during the last three weeks I have had no time to write letters. I have read the newspapers, tried to be patient, and been up to Paris. That 's my life.

We have had lovely hot weather and everything is growing well. Still, in spite of rains in May, just after I wrote to you, which seemed to me sufficient to wet the ground, every one is yelling for rain. I confess the ground does look dry.

Yesterday nine chicks came out of a nest of thirteen eggs. I was delighted, but Amélie is disappointed. They ought all to have hatched. I recognized that, when she called my attention to it. Until then I had thought it a brave showing. I shall do better next time, or, if I don't, be wiser in speech.

I went up to Paris on June 3rd and stayed a whole week, which was unusual for me, but I had work to do there and could not seem to get back. I wish you could have seen my garden when I did. It was like a wilderness of flowers. It looked absolutely unkept, although it was clean and tidy. But no one would dream of cutting the roses when I am not here, and the *Gloire de Dijon* over the front door, and the big Pink Rover over the dining-room, had bloomed and bloomed and shed their petals until the air was full of them. The grass was high, the geraniums and pinks a mass of colour. I would not have dreamed that a week or ten days could have done the work it had, although, of course, it was hot weather.

In Paris no one talked of anything but the taking of Messines, and now that the Allies have the three heights — Bapaume taken in March, Vimy in April, and Messines last Monday, — every one is hoping for another phase of a general offensive. Wise and well-informed people say it is impossible, and the gospel of patience is preached everywhere. All the same Messines was a great affair, one of the most astounding bits of preparation the war has yet seen.

We surely needed that bit of encouragement, with all the disquieting things that are going on in Russia, and with the perpetual disturbances of the Socialists and Pacifists, who find it so hard to understand even yet that peace to-day can only be a German peace, with Germany not only victor, but conqueror. Before this war can end well all the hopes of any decency or generosity or good breeding or justice on the part of the

Germans must be wiped out of the minds of every race she is fighting. The Allies must quit talking, quit explaining their position, which is clearly known now, and get down to work. This struggle will never be settled except by guns and aeroplanes, and it is waste effort to talk about Germany until she is beaten to her knees, and until she is, though this war lasts twenty years, it will never end. As a well-known American man said to one of my friends in Paris, "Our boys must not come over here to get licked," and unless Germany is licked they will be.

Day before yesterday we began to gather cherries. They are not very plentiful, and as for prunes — almost none. However, we have enough for ourselves, and as we have almost no sugar, the scarcity is not so disturbing as it would be otherwise. But it deprives the pockets here of *sous,* and they need them.

To-day is a very hot day. It is so hot that Père left for Meaux to take a few things to market before four, and was back for his coffee at seven.

You see how we occupy ourselves here in spite of the war. At this minute, but for the newspapers, which, in the silence, we read and try to understand, and but for the soldiers in our ambulance — more sick than wounded just now — and but for such heartbreaking affairs as the air raids on London when school-children were killed, we seem at times almost as far off from the war as you are. We do *not* get used to it. No one ever will, but more and more we are beginning to understand that if war is to be we must prepare to meet all the atrocities of a nation like Germany, fighting for its mistaken ideas, and its continued existence on a wrong road. The world had no right to let itself be taken by surprise. Germany had never made any secret of her ambitions. Apart from all the military and economic books in which all her ideas of her future development and her belief in conquest have been clearly set down, no German writer on any subject has been able to escape putting the national ideas into books of no matter what nature. Even as long ago as 1861 Hermann Grimm in an article on Emerson, after prophesying one Church and one State, remarked: " But what next? The strife will then be to make this one sovereignty the Germanic, to which the Slav, the Mongolian, the Romanic, and *whatever other races are called,* shall submit," and less than twenty years later (1879), James E. Hosmer, a professor of German literature in St. Louis, in spite of an intelligent effort to deal justly with the comparative struggles of England, Germany and the States, announced his opinion that the world was slowly being Germanized. After all, who knows, if, but for this stupid war, his prophecy might not have become true? There is no doubt in any of our minds that the world had been in a way hypnotized by Germany ever since 1870. If the Hohenzollerns had not returned to the methods of the days of Hannibal, there is no knowing what might have happened. Listen to what I came across accidentally the other day, about old times when "upon their great white shields they slide down the slopes of the Alps to do battle. They have armour of brass and helmets fashioned into resemblance of heads of beasts of prey. *The women fight by the side of their husbands,* then, as priestesses, slay the prisoners, letting the blood run into brazen caldrons that it may offer an omen. Even the Romans are terrified, veterans though they are from the just ended struggle with Hannibal. Papirius Carbo goes down before them, and Rome expects to see in her streets the blond Northmen, as she had just before looked for the dark-skinned Numidian. Caius Marius meets them, 100 B.C. in southern Gaul, and again in northern Italy, the front rank of their hosts — that they may stand firm — *bound together man by man, with a chain, and the fierce women waiting in the rear with uplifted axes to slay all cowards.* But Marius comes off conqueror from the corpse-heaped battle-fields, and Rome has a respite!"

I have always told you, the world does not change, — and how more than true it is that history repeats itself. Our age and time has been deaf to the warnings of the past, and blind to the writing on the wall. Yet even that is the virtue of a failing. It is dangerous to think too well of a people, but it is, after all, a generous fault. Germany's is the reverse — she thinks too ill of every one but herself, and knows herself as little as she knows other people.

If you have handy a book containing Grimm's essay on Frederick the Great and Macaulay, do read it, just for phrases like this:

"That a German should write a history of France, Italy, Russia, or Turkey would seem no wise unsuitable, or contradictory, but imagine an Italian, Frenchman, or Turk writing a history of Germany! If the book by chance imposed on some innocent mind because written in a foreign language it would only be necessary to translate it."

Well, by their own acts they have impeached themselves — and late as it is, it is lucky for the world that it is not later.

I suppose it will not be long now before our boys begin to arrive, but I have no mad expectation of their being fit for action before the end of the year, if they are then. Kitchener's first mob was dressed for the field in eight months, but England is nearer than the States, and the submarines were not so active in 1915 as they are now. It is not only a long way to Tipperary — it is a mighty long way to New York. The only prayer I ever feel like saying these days — and even that is against my habits, for I don't believe as much in asking for things as I do in being grateful for them — is: "Hurry up, America! May the Allies hold out until you get here."

Though I say so little about the war, and although we keep on doing the little ordinary things of everyday life — we must, you know — our hearts are all out there in the north, where, since the so-called strategic retreat some of the toughest fighting in the war has written Craonne, Tête de Condé and Chemin des Dames in letters of fire on our memories. The beginning of these things happened 'way back in April, but the news we get is so meagre in details that it is only now that we realize all the heroism of the effort, or are able to put a proper name on the battles. Of course we did get the news of the wonderful English work at Messines eight days ago, at once. That was such a noisy affair that it could not be kept out of notice, besides it had been preparing for so long, and was so soon over. I am told they heard the explosion in London, when the long-prepared mines were touched off. It was one of the things we did *not* hear here.

Well, Constantine is off his throne,—another wandering crowned head to be a political danger to the future. At any rate it will protect us from getting a blow in the back down there, though it comes at a late day. Next!

V

July 5, 1917

WELL, the first of our boys have marched in the streets of Paris.

I did not see them. I was not able to go up to town, nor was I in the mood to see such a procession. So in honour of the day — it was July 4th — I put up all my flags, and waited to hear about the enthusiasm with which the boys were received, from other people.

The day before, Pétain had addressed the French army in these words:

"To-morrow, the anniversary of the Declaration of Independence of the United States of America, the first American troops to land in France will march in Paris. Soon after they will join us at the front.

"Salutations to our new comrades in arms, who, without *arrière-pensée* of money or conquest, inspired simply by the desire to defend the cause of justice and liberty, have come to take their place at our side.

"Other divisions are preparing to follow them.

"The United States of America is prepared to place at our disposition, without regarding the cost, her soldiers, her factories, her ships, — the entire resources of her country. They are inspired by a desire to pay a hundred-fold the debt of gratitude they feel to Lafayette and his comrades.

"With one voice, on this Fourth of July, let the cry go up from every point on our front 'Honour to the great Sister Republic! *Vivent les États-Unis!*'"

The order was obeyed with spirit. It was one great echo of the cheers that split the air in April, and yesterday America owned Paris. One of my friends who was there wrote me last night: "I wonder you did not hear the cheers on the Hilltop. The walls of Paris shook with them. And Pershing had tears rolling down his cheeks as he rode through the shouting crowds."

I would have liked to know what he thought of Paris, as the capital of an invaded country. I am afraid it will prove a terrible temptation to our boys, for there is no question that Paris has a charm which few can resist long. I guarantee that before long the States will hear all sorts of tales about the unlicensed acts of our boys in their first encounter with an atmosphere so new to them, and a people so strange to them. Don't let that worry you. It is a phase which was to be foreseen, and was logically impossible to prevent. A large percentage of our boys — whose last thought was that they would ever be soldiers sent to fight on foreign soil—know nothing about the French. They have all heard of Paris as a "gay city," where wonderful things take place, and of France as a country where things are permitted which would not be tolerated at home. You know no race belies itself in its light literature as the French. And it is the light literature which is the most known in translations. To judge by that, women are never virtuous, men are never loyal, and we all know how often it has been said that "home" has no equivalent in French because the thing itself does not exist here. You and I know France better than that. We know that nowhere in all the world is home life more beautiful, or family ties stronger than where the words "*ma mère*" are sacred, and where father and son are not ashamed to embrace in public. If there is less hypocrisy of speech and opinion about some of the natural incidents of human experience than exists in some other parts of the world, those who draw too quick conclusions from that will be liable to find themselves mistaken. If the French make less fuss than we do about certain accidents of life, it is to their credit, and they are only a bit in advance of the rest of the world—in the vanguard of advance—in fact the banner-bearers, as they always have been, of civilization. Then, besides, you know, and the world will know when this is over, that the so-called "emotional French" are less hysterical than we are.

So don't you worry over any of the tales about the American boys in Paris which are sure to go across by cable and special correspondents. Over here our boys will grow into self-reliant, self-respecting men. They will be broken of many of the bad habits which we have to know exist, and they will go home — such of them as return — to build up a new type of American. Hardships will model their faces, which when I was last in New York looked too round and pudgy; exercise will harden their frames which were too *molle*. In fact, they will be in every way the better. They will leave a great heritage to the future and make a race with a right to pride. Besides, they will complete their education in a way that no university could, and, after it is over, no one will be able to accuse us justly again of being "a race of provincials."

I felt that I had to say this quickly, as judging by the letters I got to-day the Americans have given Paris a shock, and the material is too good to be long neglected by the space writers. So don't worry. It is unimportant.

I have another brood of chickens — this time twelve out of thirteen, — and yet Amélie is not content. I hope the next will be really satisfying, — expect them in a few days.

I don't need to tell you that I was very popular here on the Fourth. Every one treated me as if I were the entire United States of America. After long years of doubting, it was a fine feeling. I felt all warm and comfy about my heart. I had waited so long for it.

VI

July 27, 1917

I WAS surprised on looking in my letter-book to find that it is already three weeks since I last wrote to you. But a farmer's life is a busy one, and we have had strange weather — so changeable. The seventh and eighth were hot and muggy, the ninth like a chilly autumn day, the twelfth and thirteenth were very hot; on the seventeenth we had a rainstorm that turned my garden into a lake, and the road into a brook. Then came one awfully hot day — just scorching — and since then it has been beautiful. All this has been good for our crops. I've had peas and beans, cucumbers and tomatoes, strawberries and raspberries — in fact I think every day, as I sit down at noon, that I live just as well now as I could at any crack restaurant in the world. Next week I shall have green corn and all sorts of other dainties. It is a pity that it is not summer every day in the year.

On the tenth I saw the first *camions* full of Americans going over the road towards Meaux. As I sat in the little cart watching them go by, I did wish I could tell them that I was an American, but it seemed best not to. They are — for prudential reasons, — advised not to talk to strangers, and it is wise. So I contented myself with smiling at them — every one does that — and feeling a bit chagrined that they did not recognize in me a fellow citizen.

All the *commune* has been busy for a fortnight picking *cassis* — the black currants — and the English are going to risk buying them to make jelly for the soldiers. It is always one of the prettiest times of the year, when little children as well as men and women are sitting on low stools under the laden bushes, in the hot sun and the showers. But it is weary work, and they look so tired, as at four o'clock they rest for a bite and lie sprawled everywhere to eat their bread and cheese.

We have had some trying days, days when leading a normal life seemed absurd. On the seventeenth the bombardment was so heavy that the very house shook, and the twenty-first was no better. Yet the newspapers gave no news that would seem to explain in either case. It simply recalls to our minds that it is going on always, — this war.

Last night was a hard one. I was reading in bed, and, for lack of anything new, I had taken up Benson's "Lord of the World" — more interesting now than when I first read it. Suddenly I was literally made to jump out of bed by a terrible explosion — not in the direction of the front. I went into the back of the house and looked out towards Paris. It was a black night, — no moon, no stars — and deathly still. I was finally almost convinced that it was a terrible and solitary clap of thunder. So I went back to bed.

Half an hour later came a series of terrific explosions. So I wrapped up and went out into the orchard.

I could see the light of a fire in the east, but not in the direction of Paris, and much nearer. By this time I heard voices everywhere and knew that other people were up. There was no doubt what it was, of course — ammunition works. The morning papers announce the hand-grenade factory at Claye destroyed. Pity! We need all our ammunition.

Of course that meant no sleep for me. Once I am waked up well, no hope of sleeping again these days.

I am amused at your letter about Jeannette. Glad you enjoyed her, but rather sorry you ask for news of her. Alas! her news is not good. But here it is. Jeannette could never be cured of the habits of her youth, — for which she was not to blame, — nor be reconciled to lack of liberty. As long as she remained, she continued to b-l-lart in the most heartrending manner if she was left alone.

Amélie had something to do besides sitting with her, and I grew weary, if ever I sent Amélie on an errand in the afternoon, of either listening to her heartbreaking calls, or taking a book and a camp chair and bearing her company. When we did not go to her, she cried and would not eat. So pretty soon she went dry,—then—*she* went away, too. I hope she found Pierre and Paul in the Happy Hunting Grounds.

It was a pretty sore subject for some time. But one gets used to everything, and the other day I asked Amélie how much she got for Pierre and Paul. "Eighteen francs," she replied. Then I made a heartless calculation. "We paid twelve for Jeannette. We sold the whole outfit for thirty-five. We were twenty-three francs to the good plus experience, a few quarts of milk, and some fun."

I should not have diverted you with details like that. You brought it on yourself.

These bucolic diversions do not help us to *forget*—nothing can—but they sometimes ease the strain wonderfully.

Incidentally,—I saw a soldier from one of the ambulance corps the other day, who was at Arras when the battle ended after a month of pretty stiff fighting. He tells me it is a dead city. It was bombarded in the early days of 1914. It was bombarded in July, 1915, and now, through the month of

May, the battle raged round it. It was a beautiful and historic city — full of wonderful old buildings. It is now a ruin. But as the stretcher-bearer said: "Talk about beauty! I stood in the *Petite Place,* in the moonlight, one night, looking toward the once majestic *Hôtel de Ville* above whose arch-supported Gothic façade soared, in October, 1914, that lofty belfry. All about me was ruin, and through the broken façade and falling tower the white moonlight streamed, making one of the most wonderful pictures I had ever seen. It was the very majesty and dignity of desolation. No centuries-old Greek or Egyptian or Roman ruin ever moved me more deeply. I have been often in the moonlight to look at the Coliseum at Rome, and I could not help wishing that before that ruin is restored all the world might see it as I saw it that night. Its dignity, its desolation, and its beauty seemed to me so symbolic of France of to-day."

VII

August 14, 1917

SORRY to tell you that the weather turned nasty in the last days of July. The leaves began to turn brown, to dry, and to fall. The world already looks like autumn. It fills me with misgivings for the winter. I have been putting in wood, in the hope of having something I can call a fire. I have been buying wood wherever I could get it. It is slow work, the wood is queer stuff, — what the trade calls "*bénéfice des boucherons*," — that is to say, gnarled pieces, roots, big chunks, in fact all the wood not considered good enough for a respectable woodpile, and which dealers do not buy. Needless to say that I pay just as much for it as if it were the neat three-feet-long logs my fireplace demands.

There is no coal in sight.

However, it is not yet winter. It is indeed two months before, under usual climatic conditions, I should think of needing fires. Yet, even to-day I could enjoy a brisk fire in the evenings, which are more like October than August.

Don't imagine that I am depressed. I am

not. I am simply, by force of habit, telling you the truth.

I wonder if a full realization of the situation over here will ever come to you in the States. I don't yet see how it can. The ocean is wide. I know myself how difficult it is to arrive at an actual conception of a far-off disaster. But I suppose that, next year, when every day's newspaper will carry its list of casualties, you will feel quite differently from what you do now, and have less taste for the sight of marching regiments and bands of music.

Just imagine what France is like to-day. The north-east is a devastated battle-field. The rest of the country is spread pretty thick with factories making war materials. The fields on which we are depending to live are being cultivated, short-handed, as best they can be, by women, children, old men, and war prisoners. The south and west are overcrowded with training camps, *cantines,* hospitals and refugees. It is an inconceivable situation. One has to see it to realize it. When one thinks of it seriously, is n't it remarkable to see how, with the entire able-bodied male population in the war, the work of the nation can go on at all? It is not astonishing that we lack things. It is miraculous that we get on at all, and that, once the army is fed, there is anything left for us civilians.

Of course we are not just now seeing anything of the war except in our little ambulance — where to-day they are mostly sick and convalescents — usually boys slowly coming back to interest in life from having been gassed. Our roads are quiet. We rarely hear more than a dull far-off booming of guns. It often sounds about as much like horses kicking in their stalls as anything else.

To be sure we only have to cross the Marne into Meaux to get a different impression. For Meaux is a military centre, and always was. Its huge barracks near the cathedral gave it, even in peace time, a military aspect. There is to-day a big military hospital in the barracks, which are built quite round the great sunlit inner court, and cover an immense tract of ground. In the barracks there is to-day one of the hundreds of English *cantines* that the British are running for the French soldiers. It is conducted by a group of British ladies, one of them a cousin of Lord French, a lady older than I am, who works with all the enthusiasm of a girl, and with the tact and ability that girls lack.

These wonderful British women are among the most interesting things the war has brought to France. The leaders are often women — wives and widows of officers — who have seen Indian service. You know the type of horseback-riding women, used to adventure and danger, with pluck as well as charm, slender, nervous, and untiring.

Their *cantine* at Meaux is a model one. It serves special régimes for six hundred soldiers, provides reading matter, teaches them sports, takes an interest in them when they go back to the front, and keeps them furnished with all sorts of comforts.

I wish that you, who have such a respect for order — you know you always were tiresomely orderly — could see that huge kitchen, all freshly painted pale green, with its wide doors opening into the big sunlit court, where the soldiers sit about, the horses are exercised, huge army camions are lined up, and at the far end of which are the neat freshly built sheds for the German prisoners.

There is a great range across the back, and near the open door there is a reading-table on which there are always fresh flowers, and groups of rattan chairs stand around it. At one side is a tiny dining-room where the directress of the *cantine* and her aides eat, and behind it a room with two stoves where they make gallons and gallons of tea and coffee in the biggest urns I ever saw.

The service is no glorious one, I can tell you. There is nothing picturesque about it. It is sheer hard work — at times it is almost menial. I am telling you about it, because I want you to realize what war is demanding of women to-day.

Every day one of these women gets an order from the head nurse for a certain number of soups, a certain number of meat dishes, so many dishes of specified vegetables, etc. This list is written on a big blackboard fixed on the wall beside the stove, and at a certain hour the men who distribute the food come to the kitchen to carry away the trays. Often the only help they have is from the convalescent soldiers and German prisoners. They stand over the hot stoves themselves, unmindful of complexion or hands.

Whenever I was there I always felt a great curiosity regarding the mental processes of the Germans. I watched their quick way of working, their silence, their docility, and, as far as I could see, perfect politeness. I got the idea in my head that, no matter what they might say, there was not one of them, judging by their looks, who did not rejoice that for him, and probably through no fault of his, the horrors of war were over. I knew that one at least of the English ladies spoke German. So I asked her one day about them. She replied:

"They are the best, the most civil, the best disciplined help we have ever had. They are clean about their work, and absolutely obedient. There is never any question about an order. It is given. It is executed."

That did not surprise me, but that was not what I wanted to know. So I put the question flatly. "But about the war? Do they still believe in a victory for Germany?"

"Oh, absolutely," she replied. "They have no doubt about that. They say quite freely that they can easily hold out three years longer; that we may hold them, but we cannot beat them. There are no two minds amongst them on that subject. They even agree so well in their manner of insisting that it almost seems as if they were speaking under orders."

I give you this for what it is worth, only insisting, since you so often write as if you in the States had the idea that we were soon to see Germany break. I often wonder where you get the idea. Here it looks to us every year as if Germany were stronger, instead of weaker, as if each year, with her capacity for obedience and her habits of organization, she was learning in the war new ways of safeguarding herself. We never can get away from that forty years of preparation, for while we are working so hard to recover from years of foolish idleness, Germany is no more idle than we are. I have said this to you before more than once, I am afraid, and if I keep insisting it is only because it seems to me a fatal error to ignore that fact.

These ladies at Meaux, who have never before known long hours of manual labour, great responsibility, and absolute negation of personal tastes, have nevertheless started to arrange a night *cantine* at Meaux.

I may have told you before that Meaux is strangely lacking in restaurants. In spite of its historical interest, it is not as much visited as many other towns less famous. There is no restaurant of any sort in the station. There is a common *buvette* at one end where workmen go to get a drink, but where no other class would dream of entering. There is a terrace outside where one can sit down to drink a lemonade. It is just the most ordinary *buvette* with a zinc counter in front of a sink for washing glasses, and there is always a crowd — and a very smelly one — in front of it. There are a few hotels, only one fairly good, but they are in the town, at some distance from the railway station.

Of course Meaux is a great military centre now. Through its big station pass all the trains from the front from Verdun to the north which do not pass over the northern road to Belgium. Military trains are slow. Hundreds of men from the huge camp of *permissionaires* at Vaires have to change cars, both coming in and going out, at Meaux, and often they wait hours to make their connection. This wait is more often than not in the night. It is bitter cold on the long, covered platform, and there is no chance to get even a cup of coffee.

So these English ladies are setting up a night *cantine* there, to be running from midnight to four o'clock, and half the little group is to be on duty every night, ready to serve hot tea, coffee, or soup.

I often laugh when I see them, over the fuss that has been made in my time over the "eight-hour law" for able-bodied men. Of course I know that you are going to fling back at me that women are tougher than men, even harking back that boy babies are harder to bring through childhood than girls. But that has nothing to do with the question. The real thing is, that if only the world in its development could aid people to find work to do that they either loved or believed in, their hours of labour would not be the hated slavery they now are to the mass.

I hope you won't mind my talking so much about the women in this war. I wish you could come over here if only to see them. I feel that there has been nothing more worth while done in the war than the work of women of all nations. I know you women in the States are all working, but to realize what is being done, one has to see it over here.

I imagine we have buried for all time what has for so many years been known as the "woman question." It has been a long and bitter struggle, and so often conducted on unwise lines. It requires a fanatic to lead a crusade, and the woman cause has had its fanatics, — and its martyrs, too. The beauty of the whole matter is that woman has won by acts, not words. She has won by doing a woman's work. Best of all she has, for all time, given the lie to the argument that she had no right to the franchise because in case of a war she could not protect her country. It has taken a war to prove the falseness of such an argument, and to demonstrate that, while women could not, as a sex, carry a gun into battle, there was work just as important — real war work — which she could do, and she has done it well, in a manner which has compelled man to bare his head before her, and bend his knee to her just as devoutly as he ever did in the days of chivalry, even while he recognized in her a comrade and an equal.

Moreover, when she was needed and capable, she has actually gone into the firing line, and won and worn her decorations for the same reasons that men have received them.

In every branch of war work done by unarmed men, women have appeared and shown the same courage and the same unfailing patriotism as men. They have worked for the cause and died for it without in any way unsexing themselves. I have seen thousands of these women, and I give you my word that among no women I have ever met in my long life have I found "womanliness" finer than among the women near the front, every one of whom was doing work that but for them an able-bodied man would have had to stay behind the fighting-line to do.

I hope you have heard about the English Women's War Auxiliary Corps, made absolutely imperative by the need of more men before the States came in. These are young women of all classes, enlisted like men for the duration of the war, dressed in khaki, living in camps or *cantonnements* just like the men, under exactly the same conditions as the Tommies, and facetiously called by their friends "Miss Thomasina Atkins." The big force of thousands is officered by women. They live behind the lines under the same conditions as the men, and do all sorts of clerical work — post-office, telegraph, motor-cycle — in fact everything a woman can do to liberate a man to carry a gun.

I have a number of young girl friends in the corps, dressed in uniform, wearing military boots, living a soldier's life of hardship and discipline. No wonder the suffrage excitement is already ancient history. If war does nothing but this for Great Britain, it has done much. Yet we who are looking on know already that this is only one of the great things it has achieved.

This is getting to be a long letter. Never mind. When things are slow, as they are now, and I am so shut away that I have no one to whom I can chatter, no one to theorize with, I have to clear my brain now and then by talking at a sheet of paper — just to drive the haze and confusion out of my mind.

Useless to talk to you across the ocean about the ever-changing and day after day more threatening Russian situation. I am afraid nothing can now stop the fatal trend of events. For the time — and perhaps forever — we are evidently going to lose Russia. I wonder if you in the States have the faintest idea what this means? Why, if Germany succeeds in getting Russia disarmed in the next few months — well, I dare not even say to myself *all* that it seems to me to threaten. Poor Russian people — such dreamers! They are not wicked. I do not believe that they have the faintest conception of the disaster they are preparing for France. Of course Germany does not yet believe that the States can put any important fighting force into France before she fetches off the *coup* which will liberate a couple of millions of soldiers now on her eastern frontiers to march against us. It is a formidable idea for us to face. Well, England put a fighting army into France in eight months, and had to bring a large part of it from Canada and Australia. And, alas! in addition to the hordes that may come to fling themselves *en masse* on us before the States are ready, you must not forget that the middle-Europe powers can put nearly a million fresh troops into the field automatically, each year, from the classes which reach military age — they are prolific, those *Boche* races.

Then, also, no means are too low for them. When a country is without honour and without shame, its means of increasing savage purposes is tremendously increased. When the true history of the Russian *débâcle* is written, it will add another startling page to the deathless dishonour of Prussianized Germany. If one stops at nothing, one can, temporarily, accomplish many things. I am sure the untiring American war correspondent must have already told you of one of the methods by which the Germans get some of the Russians to lay down their arms. How, having, for days, bombarded a discouraged army, cut them off from their reinforcements and their commissary trains by a heavy artillery *barrage,* reduced by hunger, thirst and panic, they sent out a flag of truce accompanied by wheelbarrows full of a special kind of bread of which the Russians are fond, and *vodka* of which they have been deprived since the first year of the war. They fed and inebriated them when their hope and power of resistance was at its lowest ebb. Of course, that is not a very encouraging sign for the Russian race, but after all, as a people they are only children; not warriors, but mystics and dreamers, and know nothing of international affairs. They have never known responsibility, so how can they know honour?

It is a tragic situation for us. But we *must* be patient with them, even in our dread of the consequences. It is that, or throwing that huge, rich undeveloped country—which in the future is likely to be the Eldorado of adventurers, and see a stampede which will surpass California, or Kimberley, or the Klondike—into the greedy hands of Germany. If we cannot prevent that at any sacrifice, I do not see how Europe—or the rest of the world for that matter—is going to escape from the domination of Germany except after centuries of war. Germany seems able to fight, and organize and commercially invade, at the same time.

This is why I cannot look forward without shuddering. Germany expects to settle with Russia in the next six months. Can the States be ready then?

Don't imagine I am downhearted. I am *not*. But I tell you quite frankly, I am terribly nervous, and the calm about here just now does not make me less so. I am sure that there is not an intelligent person here who does not know what the result of this struggle is to be, but it is the realization — every month more clear — of all it is going to cost which keeps our nerves a bit overstrung.

VIII

August 24, 1917

I HAVE had quite an active month, for me. I have been visiting and I have had company twice. Rather exciting, isn't it? Otherwise my life has been as usual: — a little work in the garden, a weekly visit to the ambulance, and now and then a call from some of the convalescent soldiers.

My sweet corn came up wonderfully. I have been eating it almost every day. But you should see my French neighbours' surprise at the deed. They raise fodder corn for their cattle. They never heard of such a thing as eating any kind of corn. Whenever they pass the garden while I am gathering it, they always stop to watch me, and when I come down the bank swinging the bunch of ears in my hand, they invariably ask, "What is Madame going to do with it?"

"Eat it," I reply, opening the husks to show the golden kernels.

"*Pas possible!*" is the inevitable exclamation.

You see, if there is one thing which it is impossible to do, it is to change the habits of these people. I have cooked the corn, and shown them how to eat it. Not they! They spit it out. I *have* induced them to eat corn-bread, but only when it is made with eggs and milk, and sweetened. They call it "cake," and eat it with relish, but corn-meal mush, hasty pudding, and things of that sort, which would relieve the bread question, I have thus far found impossible for them.

Absolutely nothing happens here. After three years of war almost every day has become an anniversary day. The other years it was not so marked — this tendency to look back — but since we entered the fourth year, it seems as though every one had the same idea. It is constantly, "three years ago to-day" such and such a thing happened. First it was Liège which was on every one's tongue. Then it was Mons, and so on down the memories of that opening month of war. We are already prepared to celebrate, at the Cathedral at Meaux, and by a pious pilgrimage to the graves on the plain, the third anniversary of the victory of the Marne, a victory which seems to gain in importance each year, and which marked the end of the open field battles and inaugurated the trying trench warfare. Even when the war is over, I imagine there will have been nothing to dim the importance of this battle.

In the meantime the weather is annoying, and we have to support it with what patience we can, and try our best not to dread the winter. It is like late autumn already. I should so love a blazing fire in the evening. As it is impossible, I go into my cozy bed early and read.

We watch, as well as the reticence of our little newspapers will let us, the terribly slow and costly gnawing into the German lines — it looks about an inch a day — of the French north of Verdun, and the English east of Ypres. Now and then we get a thrilling story from some point on the line, like that of the taking of Côte 70 by the Canadians on the fifteenth, which nearly accomplished the encircling of Lens.

Quiet as we are here, we live under the obsession of the thing going on "out there," knowing that every hour is marked by its acts of personal heroism in a struggle so gigantic that the individual no longer counts, and acts of bravery are only valuable as giving tone and colour to the entire Allied effort in a war where *Man* has simply surpassed himself.

I do hope that you are reading John Buchan's "History of the War." It will help you to understand many things about which I have not been able to write you. It is not, of course, the final word. Where so much is concealed, the final word cannot be said until much later. But it is a sane and a calm effort, and it helps one wonderfully.

I refuse the bait your last letter holds out.

As long as I can resist it, I will not talk about the political situation. For over a hundred and fifty years we have made a sort of fetich of what we call "the people." Well, the justice of that idea is on trial now, and while I consider that what looks disastrous at present is really in the logical march of development, I confess that the situation is grave. Any effort to curb the movement now would be a direct attack on liberty—liberty of speech, liberty of opinion. In the advance of the world "there is no backward step, no returning," though sometimes ideas that have served their purpose do get sloughed off, and progress goes on without them.

The pitiful thing about this war is—I suppose it is true of all wars for an idea—that the bravest and worthiest have died—the cream of the younger cultured class, the best of the youth from the farming districts and fishing stations of Brittany. The cultivator has always been the backbone of France. The workingman has always been the agitator. The young farmers are all in the fighting regiments. The workmen are in the factories and on the railroads, and it is the latter class which predominates in the socialists, and has a taste for being "agin the government." The farmers are filling soldiers' graves, along with the students and the aristocracy. The workingman is filling his pockets and talking. It is a new proof—

if one were needed—of the vitality of France, the home of real liberty, where it is difficult to muzzle anyone, that things are not worse than you choose to think them. Let that satisfy you. It has to satisfy us. Besides if you will find any war, in any country, and in any century, in which some one did not get rich, from the days of conquest, even before the great William of Normandy, down to wars for an idea, like our own Civil War, I should dearly love to hear about it.

Well, my one English-speaking friend, who lives over the hill on the other side of the Grande Morin, is preparing again to return to the States. You may remember that she left here before the battle of the Marne, and returned, to my great joy, the following summer. She has a little daughter, and this is no place for a child who can be taken out of such an atmosphere. It leaves me less isolated, in a certain sense, than I was in 1914, for, in three years, my French neighbours have all been drawn closer around me by our common interests and common troubles. Be sure that I am not, and never have been at all, lonely, even though I am now and then nervous, as who is not? Your letters do not give the impression that you are absolutely calm.

IX

September 4, 1917

SINCE I last wrote, I have been travelling. I have been to Versailles for a week-end. I can hear you laughing. Well, I assure you that it was no laughing matter. The days have gone by when we used to just run out to Versailles for a few hours in the afternoon. It took me five hours and a half from my door to my destination, just at the entrance of the park, by the *Grille de Neptune*. It was a real voyage, and the first one I have made,—if you except those to Paris,—since the war broke out.

I went up to Paris by the five o'clock train, to escape the heat of mid-day. That train, which is the only one we have in these days which is not strictly a way-train, only makes two stops between Esbly, where I change to the main line, and Paris, instead of the seven the other trains make, and I expected, at the latest, to be in Paris by half-past six, with just time to get a bite, and take the twenty-five minutes past seven train for Versailles, and get there by half-past eight, before dark. No one likes to travel after dark if it can be avoided — dark trains, dimly lighted stations, no porters, and few cabs, you know.

From the beginning all my plans miscarried. The train to Paris stopped and was side-tracked three times. Once we waited fifteen minutes, so that it was half-past seven when I arrived, and I missed my train for Versailles, and had to wait until nearly nine o'clock. There were not half a dozen passengers in the train, and it was already nearly dark when it pulled out. The familiar little hour's ride was as strange as though I had never made it. The train stopped everywhere. All the stations were dark as possible, and therefore unrecognizable. It was a queer sensation to run along beside a platform in the still early darkness, see a door open from the ticket office, a woman, with a mobilization band round her left arm and a small cap on her head, come out in the narrow stream of light from the half opened door, and stand ready, while perhaps one person got out and no one got in, to blow her little whistle for the train to go ahead, while I strained my eyes to catch somewhere the name of the station, and never once did it.

If anyone had told me that anything so familiar could be so unfamiliar I would not have believed it.

The result was that instead of getting to Versailles at half-past eight, when I was expected, I got there at ten. There was no way of sending word — no telephonic communication is possible, and telegrams take often forty-eight hours for the shortest distances.

At Versailles the porter was a quarter of an hour finding a cab, so I arrived at my destination; a strange house, whose noble staircase was pitch-dark — and I had no electric lamp in my pocket — the *concierge* in bed, and very cross at being wakened, and I groped my way in the strange house up three flights of stairs to find my hostess lying awake and worrying. You see there is one thing to be said for these war times, — the very smallest effort one makes becomes an exciting adventure — else what would I have to write you about?

I never saw Versailles more beautiful.

The house in which I visited had a balcony overlooking the *bassin de Neptune.* The situation was ideal, not only for its beautiful outlook and its wonderful afternoon lights, but because of the ease with which one could, in five minutes, walk up to the top of that glorious terrace, on the park side of the palace, and look down that superb vista over the *tapis vert* to the glistening canal beyond, and also because I could sit on a balcony overlooking the street and that part of the park, and enjoy such a picturesque and changing scene as the Versailles of our days has never known.

The town was full of training camps, *cantonnements,* and *cantines.* Soldiers of all nations, all colours, all divisions, and all grades pass in and out the Park gates all day. The tower of Babel could have been nothing to what the Park of Versailles was that Sunday that I was there. There were Americans and British,—Canadians, Australians, Egyptians, Indians,—there were French and Senegalese, and Moroccans; there were Serbs and Italians; there were Portuguese and Belgians and Rastas, and alas! there were a few Russians, for there are millions of them just as ashamed of what is happening out in the east as we are, and just as sad over it. There were blacks and whites, yellows and reds and browns. There were *chic* officers, some of them on leave, still sporting their *pantalons rouges,* and much braided *képis.* There were slouching *poilus* in their baggy trousers and ill-fitting coats, and smart English Tommies, and broad-hatted Yanks, looking as if they wished they could go coatless and roll up their sleeves—it was a hot day—instantly distinguishable from the wide-hatted Australians and Canadians. Nothing was handsomer than the Italians with their smart, half-high hats, or more amusing than the Belgians' little tassels of all colours jigging from the front of their head covering. All day that picturesque crowd passed in and out of the park, with crowds of women and children and all sorts of civilians.

Just opposite the balcony where we sat was a shop where they sold all sorts of souvenirs of the town — and post cards. From morning till night the crowd stopped there, and it seemed to me that pictures of Versailles must be going over the world, and surely to many places that had never heard of it before. I could not help thinking of the beginnings of culture that all these people must be unconsciously taking in at the pores, — at least I hoped there were. Many of the boys from the States, who in the ordinary course of normal life could never have hoped to see the place, and who are able to appreciate it and love it, will at least have that much to the good — among many other things — when they go home.

Of course the palace is hermetically closed. It has to be. All the same, I did wish that some of the American boys, who had never crossed the big pond before, could have seen it. However, for actual eye satisfaction the outside of the big palace and its parks is more important. I only regretted the interior because I longed for them to have it all.

It was wonderful how gay the crowd was, and how well the soldiers behaved, and how interested they all were in the children. The interest seemed mutual. I'll warrant there is not a child in Versailles who does not know every uniform on sight, or who does not recognize every nationality and every grade.

I only saw our boys at a distance as they came and went. But my hostess, who is living in Versailles for the summer and autumn, not only meets and talks with them on days when the park is not so thronged as it is on Sundays, she has them sitting by her fireside to drink tea. She tells me that some of them are terribly homesick. They miss their women-folks, and their young girl friends. That is perfectly natural, for the comradeship between young men and women in the States is a sort of relation which no other people have or understand. Even homesickness which will be forgotten as soon as they are actively "in it" is, I am told, doing them good. It may console all of you on the other side of the water to know that the boys speak of "home" as probably none of you ever heard them speak, and say "mother" in a tone quite new to them. So there is gain in all things.

I did not care to go into the park in the crowd. It was much more interesting to watch the moving throng from my high gallery seat, and to wander about the park in the early morning, when it was practically empty. That is a chance one rarely gets unless one is staying there. You have no idea how lovely it looks then, and one can wander at will, and every turn is a new picture, all the more beautiful for lacking fellow creatures in modern clothes. I never see it, as I saw it one breezy morning, when there seemed to be only us two about, without feeling a debt of gratitude to Louis XIV, great builder that he was. It is a debt that accumulates. Even Republican France can afford to be grateful to him, and forgive his faults for the sake of the grandeur he conferred on them, and which no republic can ever dare to imitate out of the country's purse.

I wish you, who know the park so well, could see it this year. There are no flowers. Some of the pines and cedars on the terraces are neglected — the number of gardeners is insufficient for all the work — and in some of the more primitive parts of the park the trees need trimming. Instead of flowers there are vegetables planted everywhere. All the flower beds surrounding the grass plots are planted with potatoes and beans and simple garden stuff. As the French gardener is incapable of doing anything ugly, these beds of vegetables are laid out just as carefully as if the choicest flowers from the *serres* were there; each bed has its label, carefully placed, to indicate the variety, bearing the words, "Planted for Ambulance No. ——." Is n't that a pretty idea?

Several of the fountains were being repaired the morning we walked there alone, and one of them was playing, just as if for us. It was delightful to be walking along a shady alley, with the thick carpet of dry leaves rustling under foot, and stirring all one's memories of the historic days of the ancient régime, and to see suddenly at the end of the vista a jet of water rise into the air, and the autumn breeze shake it into spray. Ordinarily on days when such a sight is possible, a great crowd prevents one from realizing that it is beautiful as well as spectacular, and the same crowd and its movement drives away the spectres of the past.

It was lucky I made this brief visit. If I had not, I don't know what I could have written to you about. It is the same old story of patient waiting,—of trying realization that we are all used to of the slow movement and the meagre results. The Allies are holding the beast by the throat out there, and it begins to look as if that were about all that could be done until the boys from the States are ready to go in and choke him. After all, it is a pretty big job—and the beast dies hard. I am afraid he does not yet realize that he is being choked. All I pray is that he does not get away, and make another bound. Not that it will matter except to make us all mad.

X

October 4, 1917

SEPTEMBER was not a bad month, except that it led us nearer to the winter, which I frankly dread. In two weeks it will be time to light up the fires, not for the cheer to my eyes, but from actual necessity, — and I 've no fuel.

Already the garden is faded. The only things still flowering are a few brave roses, zinnias, and Indian pinks. Everything else has been either cut back, or taken up.

I have done nothing this month — except the usual thing, studying a map of the front, or wondering at what date Germany will choose to fling the concentrated forces the Russian *débâcle* put at her disposal against us. You seem to have not the smallest idea of this possibility, since I note in your last letter your remark "that Germany is in a shocking state, and must break soon." I wonder where you get that impression, and wait for the moment sure to come, when your eyes will be opened to the truth, — that time serves Germany as well as it serves us; that if we are stronger to-day than we were in 1914, so is she; and that not until the States can actually put *fighting men* into the line is there any hope of our doing more than we have done so far — hold the *Bœche.*

Please God the time does not come when we cannot.

Since I last wrote you I have made two trips across the Marne to Juilly, to visit the American hospital. Many of the nurses over there have been very neighbourly since, nearly two years ago, after the first offensive in Champagne, two of them led Colonel Pelletier over here one dreary rainy day to call. He is General Pelletier to-day. He gave his right arm to his country in that autumn fight of 1915, and you may know him by name in the States, as he was the first man to greet General Pershing when he landed in France. He speaks English as well as we do, — the case with so many colonial officers. Ever since that afternoon I have had a sort of sentiment for Juilly. The nurses and doctors have been rather neighbourly, but I have never got up the energy to return their nice visits. I liked the idea, that, not far away, men and women of my race were working for France, at a place that I could almost see from my lawn. I can actually, on a clear day, see Monge, the last town passed on the road to Juilly.

It was not until I had two reasons to push me that I made up my mind to go to Juilly.

First, Mademoiselle Henriette, whose

service in our ambulance had deprived her of all recreation, was anxious to see a big modern war hospital, and I had it in my power to gratify her.

Second, I had an old friend — a priest — who is a professor in the Collège de Juilly, part of which has been given up to the hospital. This Abbé, not unknown in Boston, — he once taught there, — had marched away, with a gun on his shoulder, in the days of September, 1914, but later, being delicate, it was decided that he was more useful as a teacher than as a *poilu,* and he sadly took off his tunic and resumed his *soutane.*

The first visit led logically to the second. Mademoiselle Henriette talked so much in our modest little ambulance at Quincy of all the wonders she had seen at Juilly, that our *Médicin-Chef,* a clever Russian, was anxious to see it, and I returned to introduce him and the directress of the ambulance, who is the wife of our Mayor. I made both visits inside of ten days.

You will begin to think that I am always gadding. Well, it has been rather exciting for the old lady these last weeks. I am afraid that I was getting garden-bound, just as the army is getting trench-bound, and, as ruling passions are strong in death, in spite of myself, my visits to Juilly took on a sort of before-the-war historical-research spirit.

The Collège de Juilly, which has given

up its dormitories to the hospital, is an historical university founded by the Orateriens, and situated in one of the most extensive and picturesque parks in the department of the Seine and Marne. It was in that college that Stuart kings of England educated their male offspring. There the Duke of Monmouth, the over-ambitious and popular, beloved son of Charles II, who made an almost successful attempt to crowd his uncle off the throne, was brought up, and there, also, the most brilliant son of James II, — the Duke of Berwick — whose mother, Arabella Churchill, was a sister of the great Duke of Marlborough, got his education, to which he did much honour. Perhaps it was a pity that he was the illegitimate son. English literature would have lost much of the romance that Charles Edward and Bonnie Prince Charlie inspired, but then also there would have been no German blood in the English reigning family. But perhapses are stupid.

We went out the first time in a rickety *taxi-auto,* furnished by the woman at Meaux who had taken me out on the battle-field in December, just after the battle of the Marne. We went by way of Mareuil, through Meaux, to take a Senegalese, who had been nursed in our hospital, back to his *dépôt,* and from there, by the *route* Senlis, across the battle-field, towards Supplets, where it began on September fifth.

It was a lovely day — sunny, under a pale blue sky, silent, with just a puffy little breeze. The roads were deserted, as we ran along through the wide fields. The only signs of life were the big ploughs turning up the ground for the winter wheat planting, — huge ploughs drawn by four and sometimes six great white oxen, moving slowly in the foreground, in the middle distance, and silhouetted on the hilltops against the sky-line, guided by tall, sturdy, blond youths, in white blouses, with a red band about their round caps — German prisoners. Their air was as placid as that of the big oxen they were driving, and the glance they turned on us, as we joggled by in our shaky taxi-cab, was as mildly indifferent as that of their beasts. There was no one in sight to guard them — there was no need. I am told that, as a rule, they have no desire to escape — that is to say, the common soldiers have not. With the officers it is different. Many of them would get away if they could on account of their careers. But the common soldiers are good workers. They are treated well. The fields of France are better than the trenches and butchery.

I am not going to describe the hospital for you. Don't think it. You, with your fifty-page Sunday newspapers, and your numberless magazines, get all of that sort of thing which is good for you.

I am afraid that Henriette was even more impressed by the nurses and the orderlies and the stretcher-bearers than she was by the wonders of the hospital equipment. She thought the American girls "so handsome, and so smart," and they were, — but, most of all, at tea in the huge white refectory, she was impressed by the *cameraderie* between the men and women, as they sat together over their tea. She had never seen anything like that before in all her life. She thought it charming — wished the French could arrive at it, — and declared the American women the luckiest in the world, and I suppose that she is not far wrong.

Some time in the future I shall take you to Juilly. You will not see *poilus* done up in bandages, or walking on crutches in the winding streets of the old village, or lying on their mattresses in the sun in the gardens, or sitting about in the park. You will not see the pretty picture which we saw from the window of the Abbé's study — a white-robed, white-coifed nurse, sitting on the pedestal of the tall statue of Sainte Genevieve, with her white-shod feet sticking straight out in front of her, and her young head bent over a writing-pad, while the setting sun flecked the white figures with shadows from the moving leaves of the big trees about her. I felt as if a sculptor ought to do her as symbolic. *Monsieur l'Abbé* remarked, "She *ought* to be writing verses, but I presume she is only writing home." I felt myself that the home letter was more appropriate, and felt it a pity that the home people could not have seen the picture—the tired young nurse, perhaps just escaped from the operating-room (into which I had been allowed to peep, because the doctor I had hoped to see, and one of the nurses whose visit I was returning, were there, done up in gauze, and unrecognizable,—), to write home in the beautiful, stately, historic park, at the feet of the patron saint, whose faith had turned back the Hun of ancient times, and whose Paris the *poilus* of to-day defend. But, though you will not see *that,* you are sure to find many reminders of the war days, in addition to the portrait of the well-known American woman who founded and sustains this great hospital, and which will for all time hang there, with the portraits of the great men whose names have been associated with the college since its foundation. The great park, the wonderful library, the famous Salle des Bustes, the charming dining-room with its carved wood walls and heavily carved doors, and the terraced park, with its noble trees and historic associations, will be all the more attractive because it has been the scene of a fine American effort, because American doctors and American nurses have for three years already paced its hall, keeping vigil by night and day, and rested their tired nerves in the peaceful alleys of great trees, adding their mite — and one of the noblest — not only to the history of the place, but to the cementing of the *entente*. I speak of the Americans, but the nurses are not all American. There are British, Canadians, and Australians, and there are Belgians and French, and I don't know how many nations represented in the personnel of the hospital. And as they have served the civilian population as part of their work, Juilly will never again be just the sort of place it was before the war, — for that matter, no place over here will.

We made our return by a shorter route, through Trilbardou, and across the Marne at Ile de Villenoy, into Esbly. The bridge across the Marne was one of those destroyed in September, 1914. The old bridge was of stone. The new one is a temporary one of wood — not wide enough for two teams to pass. It is in the form of a broken letter Z, so that when entering on one side it is impossible to see whether or not the bridge is free. There should be a guard there. Once there was, but there was none that day. It is not a frequented road. So as we made the first turn on the bridge, we found ourselves face to face with a red cart drawn by a tiny donkey. The donkey could not be backed, — anyway, he was further across the bridge than we were, — so we had to back off, and let him pass. It was rather a ticklish operation, but easier with an auto than it would have been with a horse.

The second visit was rather a repetition of the first, except that the doctor took us over in his car, and we went much more quickly, and that we had two little adventures *en route*.

The first was laughable, in a way. You know there is no real hunting season any more, and the fields are full of game. Partridges and pheasants run about fearlessly. They have forgotten the gun. Perhaps they know that Man has too much else to do with guns to bother them. It is very pretty to see the partridges running in the fields, and not flying often, when one is quite on them, — though it is such a menace to the crops. But it was a hare that we started just out of Meaux. It was going to cross the road when we rounded a corner. I think it could have made the other side, but it did not try. Instead, it started down the road ahead of us to race the car. We were going about thirty miles an hour, and the hare beat us for ten minutes — gaining all the time — until he got courage to side jump, and disappear in the field. I never would have believed a hare could make that pace, if I had not seen him do it.

The second adventure was tragic.

Just as we came in sight of Monge we saw a smashed aeroplane lying in the field to the south, not far from the road. We slowed down long enough to make sure that it was deserted. We knew it was a recent accident, as there was no one near. It was a French plane, for one broken wing displayed the tricoloured rosette. There was no one in sight when we reached it but a white-bloused German prisoner driving an ox-team in the field on the other side of the road; but as we put on speed again, we saw, coming towards us in a cloud of dust, a French military car, and as it approached we saw French officers standing, looking off, ready to spring, and knew that they were seeking for the machine. We hurried away, to learn on arriving at Juilly, ten minutes later, that the accident had been seen from the upper ward windows, and that the ambulance had been out, and brought back the two men — both dead.

Things like that do not upset one to-day as they once did. But all the time I was walking through the hospital, talking to the *poilus,* I had the dead aviators on my mind. It did seem so pitiful to have fallen to death over the peaceful sunny fields of their beloved France, under the bovine eyes of a German prisoner. To die in an air battle is a different thing from dying like that, and I could not but pity them, little as death seems pitiful to me to-day.

While I write all this — I think of the battle in Flanders, and of all that France is enduring and must endure in the reforming of her republicanism. Be sure she can do it. All the pacifist disturbances have only shown her the necessity, and meanwhile the world at large is learning how to judge a nation by the results of its efforts and not by the acts of its individuals. I suppose those who believe that the beauty of life lies in the struggle are right, but the trying part for me is that it looks so much finer in history than it does in the doing. That is probably because I have not a great and calm mind.

XI

October 10, 1917

I HAVE just come back from Paris. I went up to see what could be done to ameliorate the situation for the winter. We are to have almost no fuel. If I can keep a fire going in the kitchen and manage a wood fire for evenings in the salon, it will be about all I can do. But I have laid in, by luck, some *pétrole* — taken over from a friend who is going to return to the States, — so I have put in two *pétrole* stoves — one to heat the breakfast-table, and one upstairs, beside my typewriter, so that I can write in moderate comfort. It is not a healthy heat — but it is all I can do.

Everything is calm here, in spite of the battle going on in the north, and all the political excitement in Paris.

I am sure that the American papers are giving you all the details of the excitement stirred up by Léon Daudet. I can only hope he has not gone off half-cocked. The papers give us no clue to the facts of the case. Unluckily, in all three of the principal books which Daudet has published since the war broke out, — all rich reading, — he has been so unbridled in his attacks on so many prominent people, — literary, mondial, and political, — that I can't help trembling. The sort of attack he has often made on people about whom I know something does not inspire me with unquestioning confidence, although I know that almost anyone put under the microscope might give some such record as Daudet gets with his humorous, often ugly, southern temperament. No one questions Daudet's patriotism, although he is an unqualified royalist, — but then, every one has always known that. It is the policy of his paper. However, if the hearings — now secret — are over and the most dangerous, as well as one of the most brilliant, unscrupulous and wicked men in Paris, — is caught in the net, I shall feel that the excitement, unfortunate and untimely as it is, has been worth while. I cannot help feeling that, in a sense, this is only the third act of the Calmette-Caillaux affair which preceded the war, in which Calmette was killed — the first of his party "*mort pour la Patrie*," as much as if he had been killed on the battlefield. I suppose there is no such audacious man in France as Joseph Caillaux. But whether he is innocent enough to escape *always* is the question.

It is rather a pity that France should have to operate upon this ulcer in war-time. But the sore has been gathering for a good while, and I suppose the sooner it is attended to in a public clinic the better for the country, — army, government, public service and all. It will probably empty out a lot of people whom public life — or life at all — will not know any longer. You can't deny that it takes a plucky nation to gather round an operating-table at such a time — if they do, and I believe they will.

The streets of Paris are full of American boys in khaki, sombreros, and new tan gaiters, and all behaving as if they were here for a sort of glorification. In a sense it is a big adventure for them, and for some it will be "*the* big adventure" — to come over the sea, all dressed up in new uniforms, to walk about the streets of Paris, before going on "out there." No one blames them for enjoying it, any more than any one blames them for looking rather like the supers in a Charlie Frohman border drama. In fact every one likes them, just as they are, and the French are quite daft about them. It is a case of "love at first sight," only I am told that boys arriving after this are not likely to see Paris until they come back from "out there."

On my return trip from Paris I met a young officer from the Pacific coast, who, in the course of conversation, said to me: "It is odd. These people do not look a bit like us. They don't speak our language. I speak very little of theirs. But somehow they are like us. I felt at home with them at once, and every day I feel more at home. I don't know why it is — can't explain it."

So you see not all the boys are homesick, as I feared they were.

Speaking of them — the other day a young French officer, who is in the aviation corps in a camp near St. Nazaire, and who belongs to the fleet which goes out to meet the American transports coming into a French port, told me that his first westward flight to protect the incoming American troops was one of the most thrilling days of his life. I got quite excited myself listening to his description of the flight over the submarine zone to meet the fleet, flying so low that he could see the khaki-clad lads, in their life belts, packed on the decks, waving their caps in the air, and imagined he could hear their shouts of "*Vive la France!*"

I don't seem to be able to write about anything to-day but "our boys."

As for that, every one talks about them, and when any of the people here see them passing on the *grande route,* you would surely think, to hear the jabbering about it, that they had brought the "Glory of the Lord" with them. I hope they have.

Some of their experiences in getting our men acclimated are funny enough. For example, the friend with whom I make my home in Paris is an unofficial "aunt" to any number of American lads, the sons of her old friends and otherwise. The other day she had as an unexpected guest to dinner a youngster from the flying corps. I went out to buy a few things to supplement a war repast up to the appetite of a healthy boy, and he went along with me to carry the bundles. We ended in a cake-shop — they are not shut yet — one of the prettiest in a smart quarter, and I made a collection of things which I thought a boy with a sweet tooth would like, and could not get in camp. When I went to the desk to pay, the cashier mentioned the sum, but she added: "*Monsieur* has been eating cakes?"

Instinctively I said "No," to look round and find him with his mouth full, and another dainty poised at his lips.

"How many?" I asked with a laugh.

"How many what?"

"How many cakes have you eaten?"

"These little things with petticoats? I don't know. Three or four." I nodded to the cashier. She mentioned the price, and, as I paid it, he simply shouted: "What? You are not going to pay for those piffling little things? Why at home we always sample these things in a shop."

"But you are not at home," I replied. "We'll discuss it outside," and in the street I explained the French cake-shop system to him, to his deep amusement. He had only been in Paris twenty-four hours,—it was his first visit, and this was his first appearance in a cake-shop. He could not get over the "absurdity," as he called it.

Many of the boys down in the camps near Chalons have had the same difficulty in mastering French ideas and traditions regarding fruit hanging on trees.

You know the American boy's point of view regarding fruit in our land, where orchards are big. It is half the fun of being a boy. If the farmer catches the young marauders at work he chases them with whip and bad words, or exercises his skill in throwing stones. Boys put their thumbs to their noses, give the traditional waggle with their fingers, and cut for it.

Here in France it is a crime to steal fruit, a crime for which one can be arrested, imprisoned, or fined—and the law is enforced. Until the harvest is over one cannot even pick up an apple from the ground to which it has fallen from a tree overhanging the road, without risk of being punished. At a certain date, fixed by the *commune,* the town-crier beats his drum and announces the harvest over, and after that date, fruit not harvested can be picked up.

Of course the American boys had never heard of this when they came. They know all about it now. Some of them have had the fact very forcibly impressed on their minds, to their deep disgust.

"What," exclaimed one youngster, "we have come over to fight for these people, and they won't let us pick up an apple? What rot!" And it was just there that one young American had it emphatically brought home to him that he had not come over here to "fight for these people," but to fight for his own liberty, and that "these people" had really been fighting for him for three years, and he must hurry up and get ready to "go in it" before "these people" were too exhausted. I suppose it is absurd to put it that way, because they are far from done up yet, although if there were not something almost superhuman in them, they would be.

Here we have been occupied, all of us, in seeing what could be done to dress the children for school this winter.

It is going to be a hard winter.

Many of these serious, thrifty women have larger families than you think. We have over sixty families in the *commune* who have more than three children. There is one at Joncheroy of eight, the oldest only twelve — and three pairs of twins. They run together in summer, a dirty, gay, barelegged, barefooted troop, each in one ragged garment, doing their little chores, picking up brushwood and dragging it home, with the tiniest tot trotting after them. But when school begins, according to the French school regulations, they must be cleaned and combed, and shod, and I assure you they always are. But it is hard work. Of course the French tradition that puts all public school children into the uniform black aprons is a great help.

In the three years since the war broke out many of these women have had to spend their savings. Many of them, with that French love of owning land of which I have written you, have invested their savings in that way. A great many of them own an extra house which they rent for 150 fr. to 250 fr. a year. But no rents have been paid since the war began, and they can't eat their houses, and would die before they would sell. These are things that don't show on the surface, and no one complains. How can they when the refugees we always have with us emphasize the fact that we who have not lost our homes are lucky. So it was only when it was time for the school to open that it was discovered how many children had no shoes, and the communal *caisse de bienfaisance* nearly empty. However, the Americans came to our assistance, and the children went to school.

Our food problem is going to be a hard one. So far as I am personally concerned it is better than it was last year, for I have a greater variety of vegetables and plenty of apples, and there again the women of the

States have generously helped with condensed milk for the children and old people and with large quantities of rice and prunes and sugar and such things. So you see that far away as I am from you in this quiet place where we are always looking at the war, I can still bear witness that the loving hearts in the States are ever on the watch for our needs. If it is more blessed to give than to receive — and I know it is — there must be many in the States who are happy in these days of giving with both hands and full hearts.

Tell me, — over there, are you all forgetting, as we are, how it used to be before this war came? One thing I know, people who expect when this is over to come back to the France of before the war are going to be mightily disillusioned. The France of the old days is gone forever. I believe that all over the world it will be the same. We none of us shall get back to that, but I have faith to believe that we are turning our faces towards something much better. If we are not, then all the great sacrifice has been in vain.

It is getting cold and late, so this must answer for to-day.

I hope this time I have talked about our boys enough to suit you, though I am sure you will always be calling for "more."

XII

November 1, 1917

IT would be laughable, if it were not tragic, for me to recall how many times in the last thirty-nine months I have said "these are the worst days of the war." Well, each month takes a step forward in endurance, and each step forward bears witness to what we can endure, if we must. Possibly the future holds worse, but we don't know it.

The desertion of Russia tries our patience even here in this quiet place. What must it be like "out there"? Of course the Allies have got to show great indulgence to Russia — it is that, or flinging the nation — with its great territory, undeveloped resources and future wealth — into the hands of Germany. As it is, we can't do much except be patient with them — and arrange the matter after we get through licking Germany.

Though I know, as I have known from the first, that we were going to do it, I don't deny that I study the map to-day with a nervous dread of what is before us on the road. It becomes us to do that. I own to trembling. Why not? We've got the first results of the Russian downfall — the terrific drive on

Italy, and the loss of all they won in the spring—just so much work to do over again.

Don't imagine for one moment that I think that these things are disastrous. I don't. But there is no use denying that they are—*unfortunate,* and that the loss of so many men, so much material, and worst of all, the methods by which it is done, are mightily upsetting. It stirs still deeper the pacifist sets and the cowards—and cowardice has no race. It sets the socialists running amuck. It disturbs the army, of course, and that's the worst of it. But can you wonder? I repeat what I wrote you in a recent letter, which you evidently had not received when you wrote the one now before me—received yesterday, and dated October 5th,—about the time I must have been writing to you of my visit to Juilly,—that the political upheaval is not so important as you seem to fear.

Anyway, it has comic opera episodes. Here is one.

Léon Daudet, who, if he did not open the ball, led the most important figure in the dance, having dealt out domiciliary visits to a number of prominent politicians, in true revolutionary spirit, got the same thing wished on him. In a counter attack he was accused of preparing a royalist plot to overthrow the republic. Of course, it never has been any secret that he would, if he could. He does not love the present republic. Lots of honest French people don't. Amélie does n't. She is more royalist than the king. But though Léon Daudet is no respecter of accepted reputations, and has no bump of reverence, he is no fool, and he is a far too loyal Frenchman, and too ardently anxious for an Allied victory, to undertake any such stupid and impossible thing as a "restoration," in these days of desperate fighting. The accusation against him took the form of the statement that a depot of arms destined to put a royalist party in fighting trim was found in his office. The depot of arms was proved to be one of those ornamental panoplies in which men delight as a decoration. This contained—among other things—five revolvers of various patterns, a dagger in a sheath, two harmless weapons marked as souvenirs of a royalist plot of other days—perhaps that of Déroulède in the time of Felix Faure's death—two *coup de poing Américain,* and half a dozen old *pistolets* of ancient history—a pretty armament to equip royalist conspirators in these days of the *soixante-quinze* and the hand-grenade. Writers of comic opera ought to take notice. Paris laughed, and so would an audience. One thing is sure. Daudet has scored the first laugh. It looks as if he would score something more serious. We may see a procession of men whose faces have been more or less familiar to the public, and whose names are not unknown in New York, up against a wall at Vincennes, with a firing squad in front of them. I for one hope so, for the good of the future.

XIII

November 26, 1917

HERE we are, almost into December; one could have no doubt of it, it has been so cold, and I have absolutely no real fuel. We have actually done what little cooking there is over a fire of chips. Did you ever try to do that? I suppose you have when you camped out. That is a different thing. I 'd adore to have you see Amélie. She arrives with her felt shoes — high ones — in her sabots. She has a knitted bolero over her wrapper, a long knitted sweater over that, and a big ulster to top her off, and a knitted cap on her head. She does the cooking — such as it is — in that attire. Of course this means a fire for a couple of hours in the morning — the rest of the day no fire at all, — and cold suppers. It means going to bed with the dark, and putting on mittens to read in bed. In this inventive age, I do wish some ingenious person would devise an automatic book-holder, which would not only hold the book at any angle, according to the light needed, but turn the pages.

I 'd love to give you an atmospheric picture of what my little cold house looks like, when I come downstairs in the morning. But piercing chill — though it is actually visible — cannot be pictured.

Of course I don't expect this condition to last. I 've cords and cords of wood ordered. Some of it will come, I suppose, some day.

In all ways that I could I provided for this. I am done up in flannel. I wear nothing but velveteens, and am never without a fur. I run about out of doors all I can — only it is so muddy. I have tried every year to put sand on the garden paths, but have never been able to get it hauled from the Ile de Villenoy. If I only had had that, I could follow what sun there is about the house.

To sadden us all a little, our ambulance has been closed, as are all the formations of less than fifty beds, — question of heat and light. The tiny hospital has been a source of great interest and diversion to all of us. Ever since people knew it was here, every one of the American organizations and a great number of private people in the States have taken a kindly interest in it — the Red Cross, the *Comité pour les Blessés Français,* and so many others, like Mrs. Griggs of New York, whose name became very familiar to nurses and *poilus,* especially after she visited them. In fact, the little Quincy hospital, which always flew the Stars and Stripes on all American fête days, was by its American friends beautifully equipped and never lacked for anything.

The boys were very happy there. I can't tell you how they love being nursed in a small ambulance. There is something so much more *intime,* especially when they are convalescent, and can not only sit out in the garden, but go to their meals in the huge light refectory of the *patronage* of the town — a clean, square room, with well-scrubbed deal tables about three sides, and the wonderful cook — herself a war widow — presiding over the big stove at the other end, and all the white-clad nurses, including the directress herself, distinguished by her blue veil, presiding over the service. Needless to say, the sort of cooking they got was quite different from that possible in the huge hospitals, and they appreciated it.

Well, it is closed, alas! and its history entered in the record of the *commune.* We shall all miss it.

As its end was not foreseen, there was considerable material left over — canned food, condensed milk, as well as all the sheets and clothing. So, three days after the closing — the *commune* having politely asked my consent — the town-crier beat his drum at the cross-roads, and informed the people of the two *communes* that the wives of men at the front, war widows, and the refugees were invited to present themselves at the *Mairie* next day, when the *Maire* would distribute "*les restes des dons Américains*" remaining at the ambulance. So the Stars and Stripes were hung over the door of the *Mairie,* and the distribution was made.

No one is going to feel the *vide* this will make in our daily lives as much as Mademoiselle Henriette, who, after three years of arduous daily service, finds herself idle, and, what she minds more, dressed as a civilian.

I imagine that we shall not keep her here long. She has always consoled herself for her humble position, while longing for a front line hospital, with the fact that her work was hard. So there is small probability of her reconciling herself to idleness.

This morning I had a splendid bonfire — burned up all the asparagus bushes in Père's garden. It was smoky work, but I got warm. Now I am going to plant tulips, and pot geraniums. This last is a joke. I do it every year, but I rarely save any. I have no proper place to put them away. I have tried every place in the house and out, so you can guess at the kind of cold we have here. This year I have less space than usual, as the arrangements for the winter *cantonnements* are more extensive than they used to be. I have had to clear out the cellar on the north side, where I have always kept coal and wood, to make a place there for twenty soldiers. So, if I get fuel, it will have to go into the one on the west side, where I keep my garden stuff.

We have had no *cantonnement* yet, though there is a big one down the hill at Couilly and St. Germain.

Yesterday I saw these men for the first time. I went over to Voulangis by train, and Amélie drove me to the station. On the *route nationale* I met several soldiers strolling up the hill in a uniform that I did not know,—far the smartest French soldiers I had ever seen,—dark blue (almost black) snug-fitting knee-breeches, tight tunics, brown leggings and belts and black *bérets*. Just before we got to the foot of the hill I heard music, and as we turned into Couilly we found the street crowded, and saw, advancing from St. Germain toward the bridge over the Morin, which separates the two villages, a big military band filling the street from sidewalk to sidewalk, the sun shining on their brass instruments as the trumpeters whirled them in the air.

It was a new experience for Ninette. I don't believe she had ever seen anything like it in all her long life. As it was impossible to pass, I got out and went across the bridge on foot. I had to thread my way through the crowd, among whom were a great number of *poilus* in the same uniform, so I took the first opportunity to ask what regiment it was, to be told—the *Chasseurs Alpins*. So

I have seen them at last, and a regiment wearing a *fouragère*.

When I reached home that night — I drove from Voulangis — I found Amélie just putting Ninette up. I had left her at two o'clock. I returned at seven. When I asked where she had been, she told me that she had put Ninette in the shed at the coal man's, and followed the band to the square to hear the music, — the square is just across the road, — and that Ninette had enjoyed the music, in fact she had danced all the time, and was so tired that it had taken her nearly an hour and a half to climb the hill. I suspect that Amélie, who adores dancing, judged Ninette by herself.

The atmosphere is rather vibrating here. All this defeatist propaganda is trying to our nerves and our tempers. It is logical enough, but it is ringing the death knell of socialism among the farmers. The real truth of the tension, is, of course, the Russian situation. There has been so much sentimentality about Russia, and so much ignorance, and every day seems to bring its own special disillusion. At the time of the abdication of the Czar, the event was given considerable dignity here. Later, when the menace of the separate peace began to loom up, with its liberation not only of the soldiers on the Russian frontier, but of the supposed-to-be millions of German prisoners, optimists argued that the Germans who were in Russia at the time of the revolution would be more likely to sow revolution in Germany than docilely re-enter the shambles. Error again.

My own head gets confused at times. Can you wonder that these people about me cannot see straight? We have all blundered so. I cannot help asking myself if we shall blunder on to the end. I really get weary of hearing the peace terms of the Allies discussed. I know that it has to be, that it is absolutely necessary, since the days of secret diplomacy are over, that the truth of what the Allied nations are struggling for—and must have—should be kept eternally before the eyes of the world—lest they forget. But I long so to think of nothing but licking the Germans, and talking after that is done. There are moments when I feel that every one of us—women and children as well as men—ought to be marching out towards that battle-line—if only to die there. I am laughing while I write that sentence, for I have a vision of myself limping along, carrying a gun in *both* hands—I could not lift it with one—and falling down, and having to be carefully stood up again. We mere lookers-on encumber the earth at this epoch—the epoch of the young and the active.

There was a time when we used to talk of such things as nobility and chivalry. Both are with us still. Poets and painters, romance writers and dramatists have glorified both in the wars of the past, and shrined them under a halo of immortality. The future will do that for this war.

I am getting terribly impatient of words — of everything, in fact, but deeds. I am beginning to feel as Amélie does. The other day there was a criticism of a military operation in the English parliament, and she said, impatiently: "Well, if I were Haig I would simply reply, 'If you don't like the way I am doing this thing, just get down off your cushioned seats, and come out and face the guns yourselves.'"

She does not know whether the benches in the House of Commons are cushioned or not. For that matter, neither do I. It is a short-sighted point of view, but I often feel the same way myself.

XIV

December 20, 1917

NEARLY a month since I last wrote. So I suppose all through January I shall be getting letters of reproach from you. I can't help it, and I 've not an excuse to throw at you, — simply had nothing to write about. Things are happening every day, everywhere, but I am not writing a history of the war, and nothing happens *here*. We are simply holding on and smiling, and I suppose we shall continue to do that until the boys from the States are in real fighting trim.

The only piece of news at my house is that my little kitty, Didine, is dead, and buried on the top of a hill in Père's garden under a white lilac bush. It is absurd to grieve in these days for a cat, but he was the only affectionate cat I ever knew. I miss him terribly, especially in the evenings, when he always sat on my knee while I read.

My English friends at the *cantine* of Meaux have moved on toward the front to a place called Serche, near Baisne, in the Aisne, in the part of the territory liberated last March. There they have a wonderful foyer for two thousand soldiers, a *cantonne-*

ment—library, concert hall, tennis courts, tea rooms—in fact everything which can help the soldiers to feel at home and cared for.

I had a letter from them yesterday, telling me that they had arrived safely with their saddle-horse and their dog, and that they had a royal reception, that they had found their little house all ready,—a pretty demountable structure—for everything there had been destroyed,—painted green, and most attractively placed. The letter added, "There were flowers everywhere—even bouquets in each of our bedrooms—but, alas! there were no wash hand-bowls."

I loved that. It is so adorably French.

I am sure that you are just as much impressed as we are with the idea that the English have taken Jerusalem. Shades of Richard Coeur de Lion! Just think of General Allenby marching his army piously into the Holy City, and writing his name in history along with St. Louis and all the bands of Crusaders. Yet we are all too occupied with nearer things to do more than turn our eyes in that direction, give a thought to the stirring visions it calls up, and then mentally return to the nearer battle-field.

I am going up to Paris for Christmas. I am urged, and there seems to be no reason why I should not, or for that matter, why I should. I will write as soon as I return.

XV

January 15, 1918

AGAIN it is more than three weeks since I wrote, but this time I really am not to blame.

I wrote you that I was going up to Paris to spend Christmas. I fully intended to be back here before New Year's Day, which is the great French fête day. It was very cold when I left here, and every day the mercury dropped a little lower, until it began to snow, with the result that I was not able to leave Paris until January 5th.

I had telegraphed Amélie that I would be back on Thursday, the 27th, but the weather was so bad that it was impossible, and I sent word that I would let her know when to expect me — as soon as the snow stopped. Several days went by before it seemed wise to start, and then when I telegraphed, Amélie replied that I was to stay where I was until our roads were in better condition, that the hill was a sheer sheet of ice, and that neither the horse nor the donkey could possibly climb it.

So there I was stranded in Paris. By the Friday after New Year's, I began to feel pretty desperate, when suddenly there came a call on the telephone, and there was Mademoiselle Henriette in Paris. She said she had just arrived, and that she was going back in the morning; that the 215th infantry had arrived and was cantonned in the *commune,* that the Captain was going to send a military wagon to the station in the morning to fetch her, and that she had told Amélie that she should bring me back, if I wanted to come, and of course I did.

So Saturday at noon I was in the train, where I discovered that the wagon was to meet us at Esbly, not Couilly. Mademoiselle Henriette was a little upset when she saw my surprise. You see she is young and vigorous, and in good weather she never thought of taking the train at Couilly. She gaily footed it to Esbly, five miles away. She had not even thought how much easier it would have been for the horses to take us from Couilly — two miles of hill instead of five.

At Esbly we found the wagon awaiting us. You ought to have seen me boosted into it. I sat on a box in the back, so that the adjutant who drove and Mademoiselle Henriette could shelter me a bit, — we had no covers. My, it was cold! The wind blew a gale from the north. The road was a sheet of ice, and the poor horse pulled and tugged and slipped. The steepest part of it was through the town of Condé, and I never realized how steep that road was until I saw the horse being led and pushed up it that terribly cold day.

I reached home about frozen, to find the house looking gay, and a huge fire in the salon,—but no Amélie. They told me she had supposed we were coming by Couilly and had gone on foot to meet us, with rugs and foot-warmer. She got back about ten minutes after we did—in such a state of perspiration, lugging the big foot-warmer, full of hot charcoal, wrapped in a big carriage-rug. I expected her to fuss, after making a trip of nearly four miles on foot, carrying such a bundle. But she did not. I sat behind a screen by the fire and thawed out. In spite of the fire the house was a refrigerator. Amélie told me there had been hot-water bottles in my bed all day, as the sheets were so cold she was afraid I would get a congestion; I did not. But I slept with a hot-water bottle in my arms and a hot brick in each of the bottom corners of my bed.

The presence of the 215th makes the place very gay again. It is a crack regiment from the north. Most of the men and fully half of the officers are from Lille—men who have practically had no news from their families since August, 1914.

I had a war tea the Sunday after I got home—six officers and Mademoiselle Henriette sitting round the table — and we talked morals and history, philosophy and literature — no war.

There are some charming men in the regiment — men who in civil life are bankers, lawyers and manufacturers — almost no professional soldiers. In the ranks are some of the most amusing *poilus* I have yet encountered. For instance, there is a *bombardier*, with a gold bomb on his sleeve, though I neglected to ask what it meant. He speaks English, and when he heard that there was an English-speaking woman in the *commune* he felt that he ought to come and present his respects. He came, and gave me a few as hearty laughs as I have had since the war began.

He was a queer type. He was pure French — born in Lille of French parents, but taken to England when he was very young by a widowed mother, sent to school there, and his home is still at St. Helier, where he left a wife and baby.

I wish you could have heard him, in the broadest cockney English, tell the tale of his difficulties in getting himself enrolled in the French army.

Born in France, brought up in England, never knowing a word of French until he was out of school, he had never taken out English naturalization papers, and never intended to.

A few years before the war broke out —

at the age of eighteen, he left Jersey, and came to France to offer to do his military service. He spoke almost no French, and fell in with an officer who did not care to bother with him, as he did not seem to be very well able to explain what he wanted. He did not have the proper papers. He did not know what he needed, or how to get them. He only knew that he had arrived at the age when a Frenchman ought to be in a *caserne*. No one else seemed to care a rap whether he was or not, so he went back to Jersey, with his feelings very much hurt. He had wanted to do his duty. No one cared. So he went back to his farm, took off his store clothes, put on his blouse, and practically felt, "Devil take my native land."

Well, not long after that it looked as though the devil was going to obey him. Once more he went to Lille. Again he presented himself. This time war had begun, and he was looked upon as "suspect." How dare a man speaking English and French equally atrociously, and with no proper papers, claim to be a Frenchman? This time he was madder still. The military authorities did not know anything about him. Apparently they did want him. A sympathetic drill sergeant suggested that if he were anxious to fight there was always the Foreign Legion, and no questions asked.

"No, I'll be hanged if I do," he said to

himself. "I'll enlist in the English army." So off he went to London. But in London it was necessary to lie. If he told the recruiting officer there that he was born a Frenchman, of course he could not take him. He began by saying he was English, born at St. Helier, but he was not a neat liar, and he soon got so twisted up that he was frightened, broke down, and told the truth; explained that he had twice been to France, but as he had no birth certificate, was not even sure of the date, etc., had never lived in France since he was a baby, had no idea how to go to work to put himself *en règle,* so, as he wanted to fight, he had thought that England might take him.

The recruiting officer in London was sympathetic. He took down the facts, and told the lad to go home and wait until the matter could be straightened out. But the war was a year old before he was finally called, and entered as the rawest kind of a raw recruit.

The story itself is amusing, but you should have heard him tell it — half in cockney English, and half in barrack-room French. It was killing. I heard more words that were new to me than I have heard in an age. I wanted to stop him every two minutes, and either get a slang dictionary or call for a word-of-mouth translation. But he talked so fast, and gesticulated so that I managed to get it. I nearly upset myself trying not to laugh while he described his early days of hurried training. He visualized himself standing the first day with the contents of his *sac* about his feet, trying in vain to remember the names of all the articles, and to get them back compactly into the *sac,* from which the drill corporal had tumbled them. He was even funnier when he told about his efforts to conquer military etiquette,—to salute the proper person and recognize his rank at sight, never to salute when he had on no head covering, for every one to him was "mister" and he had never even heard of the shades in salutation.

But if he was awkward in many ways compared to some of his comrades, the moment he got a bomb or a grenade into his hand it was another matter. There he had the advantage of having played English sports all his life. I never realized that he was a fine type until I saw him giving a lesson in bomb-throwing out in the fields. When he straightened up and swung his arm into the air, I appreciated that he was a fine type and graceful.

The intense cold shows signs of moderating. My tulips are beginning to come up.

At last Caillaux is in the *Santé,* waiting to be tried for high treason. Well, it is a comfort. He ought to be left there in silence, isolated and forgotten, until the war is over. But, alas! although this is really no time for an operation on the great scandal and clearing up the terrible plotting of which he is possibly the centre, it has to be done. We have been bringing into force all kinds of laws to prevent holding him in silence. Merely the *habeas corpus* is enough. Some of our most prized reforms are inconvenient at times, aren't they?

XVI

February 1, 1918

THIS morning it looks to me as if all we have been dreading since the Russians deserted us is likely to come true. One thing is certain. The German offensive is not going to be long retarded, and what is surer still is that it is going to be preluded by a desperate German effort to terrorize the civilians, and break the *morale en arrière*. Of course that is another bit of false psychology. There is nothing which pulls the French together like a blow.

Of course you know that Paris has enjoyed a strange immunity from air raids. While England has been attacked night after night, Paris has been spared. I'd hate to tell you of all the theories I have heard exploited in explanation. I've had some theories myself. There were people who believed that the defences of Paris could not be passed by the German air fleet. I had for a time the illusion that perhaps this was true, until I was told one day by an aviator that the German fleet in the air could attack Paris whenever it was ready, and, that while aerial methods of attack had made great progress in the past three years, no method of defence was by any means a sure protection.

On dit that the reason for the persistent action against England is explained by the hesitation of the French to follow England's example and give the Germans tit for tat by attacking the Rhine towns. As the German civilians are much more nervous than either the French or English it was necessary to terrorize the latter if possible,—and it has not worked. Also, in spite of the reluctance of the French, they have lately been following England's sturdy lead. It has got to be done. The curse will fall on the nation which began it—Germany.

I imagine that, when the cable carried the news to you yesterday that, after a long freedom from air raids, Paris had been seriously attacked Wednesday night, and that the raid had lasted well into Thursday morning, you little dreamed that I had stood in my garden, and saw—or rather heard,—it all. But I did, and I can assure you that it was an experience that I never expected to have.

On Wednesday night I went to bed early. I must have got to sleep about eleven. If I do not sleep before midnight there is a strong possibility of my not sleeping at all,—one of my old-age habits. My first sleep is very sound.

I wakened suddenly with the impression

that I heard some one running along the terrace under my window. I sat up and listened, half believing that I had been dreaming, when I saw a ray of light in the staircase — my door was open.

I called out, "*Qui est là?*"

Amélie's trembling voice replied, "*C'est moi, madame*," and I had the sudden wide vision of possibilities, which I am told is like that of a drowning man, for I realized that she was not coming to me in the middle of the night for nothing, when she appeared in the doorway, all dressed, even to her hood, and with a lighted candle in her hand.

"Oh, Madame," she exclaimed, "you were sleeping? You heard nothing?" And at that moment I heard the cannon. "*Oh, mon Dieu, Madame,* what is happening out at the front? It is something terrible, and you slept!"

I listened.

"That is not at the front, Amélie," I exclaimed. "It is much nearer, in the direction of Paris. It's the guns of the forts." At that moment a bomb exploded, and I knew at once. "It's the Gothas, Amélie. Give me something to put on. What time is it?"

"Nearly midnight," she answered.

It took me less than ten minutes to dress — it was bitterly cold — and I wrapped myself in my big military cloak, put a cap over my tumbled hair, and a big fur round my neck, grabbed my field glasses, and went out into the orchard, which looks directly across the fort at Chelles in the direction of Paris.

It was a beautiful night, cold and still, white with moonlight, and the sky spangled with stars. For three hours we stood there, — Père and Amélie and I, — listening to that bombardment, seeing nothing — ignorant of what was going on. The banging of the guns, the whirring of the *moteurs,* the exploding of shells seemed over us and around us — yet we could see nothing. It only took us a little while to distinguish between the booming of the guns at Chelles and Vauclure, endeavouring to prevent the Gothas from passing, by putting up barrage firing, and the more distant bombs dropped by the flyers that had arrived near or over the city.

It was all the more impressive because it was so mysterious. At times it seemed as if one of three things must have been happening — either that we were destroying the fleet in the air, or they were destroying us, or that Paris was being wiped out. It did not, during those hours that I stood there, seem possible that such a cannonading could be kept up without one of these results. It was our first experience, and I assure you that it was weird. The beauty of the night, the invisibility of the machines, our absolute ignorance of what was going on, the humming of the *moteurs* overhead, the infernal persistent firing of the cannon and the terrific explosion of the bombs, followed, now and then, by a dull glow in the west, was all so mysterious. As the long minutes crept by, we began to notice details,—for instance, that the air battle moved in waves, and we easily understood that meant several squadrons of German machines, and we could finally, though we could see nothing distinctly, realize by the firing that they approached, met the guns of the forts—passed over or through the barrage curtain, or retired, and tried again, then, having dropped their bombs, swept more to the west, and gave place to another attacking squadron. They seemed finally to retire in the direction of Compiègne and Soissons, pursued by gun fire from the forts.

It was four o'clock when we finally went into the house, leaving silence under the stars and the moonlit night. Amélie stirred up the embers, threw on a little wood, put the screen around me, made me a hot drink and I sat there to wait for daybreak. It seemed strange to go out of doors in the morning, and see nothing changed, after such a night.

We waited impatiently for the morning papers. They contained nothing but the mere fact that Paris had been bombarded by Gothas. There had been victims and damage, but in comparison with the effort, the result had been unimportant. Out of the twenty-eight German machines which had taken part in the attack, only one had been brought down — that fell near Vaires, not far from Chelles.

This was our first experience of the sort, and I could not help feeling puzzled that so much heavy firing could go on, and out of twenty-eight machines only one be touched. But that was only my first impression. I knew when I came to think it over that it was not easy in the night to do more than try to keep the enemy off. The more I thought it over the more I became convinced that up to now there is no very effective way of preventing night air raids.

My letters which came this morning gave me some details of the raid, saying enough to let me guess what parts of the city were reached. They penetrated as far as the Avenue de la Grande Armée, and dropped bombs also in the vicinity of the Halles, and the Gare de Lyons. Every one writes that Paris is perfectly calm, although it is evident that the government — judging by the rapidity with which it is preparing systematic protection for its population, — believes this to be but the beginning of another desperate attempt to break the *morale* of the country.

There are people at Voisins who claim to have seen the Gotha that fell at Vaires. Perhaps they did. I did not.

To-day has been a chilling day. This

morning we went on bread rations — one pound a day. It is enough for me.

I have planted my climbing sweet peas. I ought to have done it in October. I don't know why I didn't, any more than I really know why I bothered to-day. One must not let one's self grow idle. I know that. But I hate having life become mechanical. The strain is beginning to tell, and I hate to feel that.

XVII

February 20, 1918

THREE weeks again. Sorry.

Mademoiselle Henriette is getting ready to go to Salonique, where nurses are needed. Ever since our ambulance closed she has been very restless, and it grows on her. She had been so accustomed to wearing a uniform, with three years' service *brisques*, on her left arm, and to feeling herself a part of the great army of defence, that to walk about in civilian clothes seems to her stupid, and I don't wonder.

Her discontent culminated the other day, when we had a very interesting *cantonnement*. The regiment arrived at nine o'clock one evening, and there was a military mass at the little church at Quincy at nine the next morning. One of the captains, a priest, and among the bravest men in a brave regiment, preached a remarkable sermon. Every one went, and of course the little church was not a quarter big enough. The soldiers knelt on the green in front of both doors, and even in the road for the elevation. It was a very touching sight. The regiment had just come out of the firing line.

Poor Henriette, in her tailored dress and hat, felt terribly out of it, — she who, a few months ago, would have been kneeling among the soldiers in her white *coiffe,* with the red cross on her forehead. She was near to tears when she remarked that no one in the regiment knew that she, too, had given three years of her life to the cause. So she must get back into the ranks, and it looks like Salonique, — a hard post, but it means sacrifice, and that is what she wants.

Thus far this month the weather has been delightful, and, though mornings and evenings have been chilly, there have been many days when I have not needed a fire, and be sure I am grateful for that.

On St. Valentine's Day I went up to Paris — just to change my ideas. I had not been up since that terribly cold spell which ended early in January. So I had not seen the city since the *big* air raid. Every one had written me details about the changed appearance of the city — details as often comic as otherwise. I was curious to see for myself. Curiosity killed a cat, you know.

Well, there are changes, of course, but one has rather to hunt for them. Everywhere — if one looks for them — large white cards are hung on doorways. On them are printed in large black letters the words "*ABRIS — 60 personnes,*" or whatever number the cellars will accommodate, and several of the underground stations bear the same sort of sign. These are refuges designated by the police, into which the people near them are expected to descend at the first sound of the *sirènes* announcing the approach of the enemy's air fleet.

More striking than these signs are the rapid efforts being made to protect some of the more important of the city's monuments. They are being boarded in, and concealed behind bags of sand. You 'd love to see it. Perhaps you have, already, for I am sure that some enterprising photographer is busy preserving the record. Sandbags are dumped everywhere, and workmen are feverishly hurrying to cover in the treasures, and avoid making them look too hideous. They would not be French if they did not try, here and there, to preserve a fine line.

The most important group on the façade of the Opera is thus concealed. You remember it,—on the north-east corner—Carpeaux's "La Danse." Of course you do, because don't you remember we went and looked at it together at the time Helène de Racowitza's suicide recalled the woman who posed for the figure of Apollon in the group—she who caused the duel in which Ferdinand Lasalle was killed, and whose affair with him inspired George Meredith's "Tragic Comedians." Poor Helène, I imagine she was a much more feeble character than Meredith drew her, but she was a beauty of the Third Empire sort, and the shadow of great men fell over her, and made her immortal as an idea, although she outlived husbands, and lover, youth, beauty, and prestige. Still, one cannot pity too much the woman over whom a famous author threw a mantle of greatness during her lifetime. It was unfortunate that she could not have lived up to it. She tried hard at the time that she wrote "Princesse et Comédienne," but the difficulty was that in her memoirs she got herself terribly mixed up with the literary portrait Meredith drew of her.

The Rude group on the Arc de Triomphe, the only real work of art in its ornamentation, has also gone into retirement, and so have the doors on the west front of Notre Dame, and famous equestrian Louis XIV groups from Marly-le-Roi, which adorn the entrance to the Champs-Elysées, and the entrance to the Tuileries garden opposite. The latter have funny little chalets built over them.

You might think that rough work of this sort would disfigure the city we love. But on my word, it does not. I really believe I love it all the better, — dear, menaced Paris. Perhaps it is because it has been and still is, in danger, that we realize anew the immortal charm. I cannot put into words just how I feel about it, but I imagine you will understand. Every one of those hoardings and all these sacks of sand seem like italics to draw my attention to how dear it all is to me. We are so prone to take the beauty we find in life as a matter of course.

Possibly you, who have not seen Paris for four years, might find more changes than I do, who have watched it all the time.

I often wonder how it would look to you, who only knew it in its better days. I have no way to establish a standard. I have seen the change, of course—but only little by little, and never losing any of the charm. If it is really much altered I don't know it. Just as one has to shake one's self hard to realize the slow changes which time brings to the faces of those whom we love, so am I unconscious of the changes the war has brought on Paris. I know that in some parts of the city there are fewer people in the streets. I know that in the centre of the city one finds still much movement, though it has changed its character. The soldiers of all nations have done that. To me it has never looked more beautiful than it does in these days. Its loveliness simply strikes terror to my heart for fear of what might be, now that the Germans are so desperate.

My visit was not altogether a peaceful one.

Perhaps I never told you that one of my Paris friends, whenever she thinks I am staying away from town too long, has a habit of writing to me, and promising that if I will come up to town they will try and arrange an air raid for me. I never had happened to be there during one. She used to say, "You really have seen so much, that it would be a pity not to be *in* one of these raids before the war ends." Of course, that was before the attack of January. Since then, there has been no need to arrange such a thing merely as experience. I have had it.

All the same; they brought it off on Sunday night—the 17th. Thank you, I did *not* enjoy it at all. It was an absolutely ineffective raid, as far as doing any damage went. But we did not know *that* while it was going on. I would not have believed that so much noise could do so little harm.

Of course the papers tell you how calm Paris is. It is. But don't let that lead you to suppose that an air raid is anything but a very nasty experience. I imagine that very few people are afraid of death to-day. Few as the air raids have been, Parisians have already learned that the guns for the defence make most of the noise. The explosion of the bombs, if rarer, is a more terrible sound. But what is hard to bear, is the certainty that, although you are safe, some one else is not.

I suppose that if I don't tell you what we did and how we passed the night, you'll ask me later, and then I may have forgotten, or had first impressions overlaid by other events.

Well, Sunday evening we had just gone to bed. It was about ten o'clock. I was reading quietly when I heard a far-off wailing sound. I knew at once what it was. My hostess and I tumbled out of our beds, unlatched the windows so that no shock of air expansion might break them, switched off all the lights and went on the balcony just in time to see the firemen on their auto as they passed the end of the street, sounding the "*Gare à vous*," on their *sirènes*,—the most awful, hair-raising wail I have ever heard—like a host of lost souls. Ulysses need not have been tied to the mast to prevent his following the song of this siren!

We were hardly on the balcony, when, in an instant, all the lights of the city went out, and a strange blackness settled down and hugged the housetops and the very sidewalk. At the same instant the guns of the outer barrage began to fire, and as the night was cold, we went inside to listen, and to talk.

I wonder if I can tell you—who are never likely to have such an experience—how it feels to sit inside four walls, in absolute darkness, listening to the booming of the defence, and the falling of bombs on an otherwise silent city, wakened out of its sleep.

It is a sensation to which I doubt if any

of us get really accustomed — this sitting quietly while the cannon boom, and now and then an *avion* whirs overhead, or a venturesome auto toots its horn as it dashes to a shelter, or the occasional voice of a gendarme yells angrily at some unextinguished light, or a hurried footstep on the pavement tells of a passer in the deserted street, braving all risks to reach home.

I assure you that the hands on the clock-face simply crawl. An hour is very long. This raid of the 17th lasted only three quarters of an hour. It was barely half-past eleven when the *berloque* sounded from the hurrying firemen's auto — the B-flat bugle singing the "all clear," — and, in an instant, the city was alive again, — noisily alive. Even before the *berloque* was really audible in the room where we sat, I heard the people hurrying back from the *abris,* — doors opened and banged, windows and shutters were flung wide, and the rush of air in the gas pipes told that the city lights were on again.

I don't find that the people are at all panic-stricken. Every one hates it. But every one knows that the chances are about one in some thousands, — and takes the chance. I know of late sitters-up, who cannot change their habits, and who keep right on playing bridge during a raid. How good a game it is I don't know. Well, one kind of bravado is as good as another. Among many people the chief sensation is one of boredom — it is a nuisance to be wakened out of one's first sleep; it is a worse nuisance to have proper *saut de lit* clothes ready; and it is the worst nuisance of all to go down into a damp cellar and possibly have to listen to talk. But, oh my! what a field for the farce-comedy writer of the days after the war. It takes but little imagination to conjure up the absurdities of such a situation that the play-maker can combine in the days when these times can be looked at from a comic point of view.

I came back from town on the 18th. I found everything quiet here. The only news is that my hens are beginning to lay — but so are every one's. While my hens did *not* lay, eggs went up to fifteen cents a piece. To-day, when I get three dozen a week, I can buy them, two for five cents. The economics of farming get me. There must be a way of making hens lay all the year round. It is to be one of my jobs next year to learn the trick.

XVIII

March 9, 1918

WELL, we have been having some very droll weather, and the weather is a safe topic, especially when you seem to read between the lines of my letters that I am getting demoralized, and at what you choose to call an unnecessary moment, with so many of "our boys" landing every week. That's all right, but though they *are* here, they are not ready, and there you are.

But weather?

I told you that February was a very pretty month. It often is in France. We had some lovely nights, when I used to go out in the moonlight, and look up in the starry dome and pick out the constellations I knew. But I seemed the only one here who enjoyed them. Every clear night seemed to offer an open road to the Gothas. It is a pity to live in a time when a lovely night simply stands for a menace. As long as the February moon lasted Amélie went home in a nervous tremble every evening. She simply hates the night attacks, although there is not the least real danger here.

The thing that torments me is the feeling

that this aerial activity presages the German offensive. We all know it is coming — our aeroplanes have announced that the Germans are concentrating their forces on our front — but when — where — on that long line? If any of them knows at headquarters, they are not, naturally, telling.

I am afraid that no one was sorry when, on the first, the snow began to fall. It lasted, off and on, five days. Every night Amélie said, as she closed the shutters, "Well, let us get a good night's rest. The Gothas cannot go to Paris to-night." When it ceased snowing, early Wednesday morning, there was a foot on the ground. But the sun came out, and by evening there was no snow at all, and Amélie was sad again.

On Thursday — that was the 7th, — I worked all day in the garden, setting out rose bushes, and though it was a beautiful night, everything was calm. But last night was a trying one. It began earlier than the one in January, and it did not last as long, but it was worse while it lasted. It was only a little after nine o'clock, and I was on the terrace, and the house was not shut up, when the first gun of warning from the forts was fired. Some one up the hill called, "What's that?" and another voice replied, "Paris."

I hurriedly closed my shutters, and put out the lamp I had just lighted, and went into the garden to watch and wait.

The battle of last night was quite different from the previous ones. This time, there were no aeroplanes in the air, except the Boches'. The forts in front of us — Chelles and Vaujours — not only used their artillery to put up a barrage, they had their searchlights on most of the time, and sent up at intervals a series of *fusées éclairantes* — so pretty as they followed one another in a line — they were usually four in a series — and now and then a rocket. It might have been fireworks — only the Gothas went right over our heads in three distinct waves, flying so low in an early evening, not at all dark, that we frequently saw them, when caught by the rockets or searchlights. We could not be sure when they succeeded in passing, but the explosion of bombs in Paris told that soon enough, while the noise of the machines over our heads told when they were actually turned back.

I must tell you an amusing thing. Amélie has always insisted that she could tell a Boche machine by the sound of its *moteur*. Perhaps she can. She says always, "Listen, now! Can't you hear that *Boche?* His *moteur* grunts just like a pig" (of course this is funnier and more significant in French — *comme un cochon*), "but ours make music — they sing!" Pretty idea? Well, the beauty of it is, I repeated it to an aviator the other day as a joke. He looked at me seriously and replied, " But it is absolutely true." Evidently I am sometimes stone deaf.

It was midnight when I came in, and that is how it happens that I am writing to you very early in the morning — just daybreak, because, I suddenly decided, in a sleepless night, that I needed a change of scene. The only one available is to go to Paris, and talk it over in English instead of French. So I am sending these few words for fear that if I am detained longer than I plan — and in these days one never knows what may happen — there will not be again too long a lapse in my letters.

Oh, I really must mention the British going to Jericho, or you will think that I have my eyes so fixed on local things that even my mental vision cannot look over the horizon line. Nice idea, isn't it — the Australian cavalry riding into Jericho? We've wished Jericho on so many people in our time that it is comforting to think that, finally, some one has really gone there — and history has recorded it.

XIX

March 17, 1918

YOUR letter just received remarks that I seem to do a deal of "gadding" in these days. Well, I told you in my last that I was going again, and I did. I went the day I wrote to you,—that was the 9th, and came back day before yesterday. Apparently I must have forgotten to tell you that, after all these months, the Commander of the Fifth Army Corps had decided to give me a *permis de circuler* good for three months. That is how it happens that I can "gad," as you call it. I am afraid that you cannot realize just what it means after years of such restrictions as I had to support, to be free to move without explaining each time, fixing the date a fortnight in advance, and then waiting in uncertainty as to whether the simple request would be granted or not. It inspires one to move on a bit, when it is not absolutely necessary, just for the joy of feeling free.

On the way down the hill to Couilly on Saturday, the day I left, we met the 89th Infantry marching in from Lagny, where they had been resting for some weeks, to canton on our hill, and I was half sorry that I was leaving, especially as air raids are of almost nightly recurrence, and Amélie, who hates them, worries when I am away. It is useless for me to explain to her that in town I stay in a part of the city which is practically safe — well to the south-west, in an apartment on the second floor of a six-story building. Bombs which fall on a house rarely go through more than three stories, and those that burst in the street seldom damage above the first floor. Amélie is always, in these days, looking for the surprising and the unexpected. I fancy she would feel happier if she could be assured that at the first sound of the *alerte* I would make for an *abri* with an electric lamp in my pocket, a camp-stool in one hand, a shovel in the other, and a pickaxe over my shoulder. Then there should be a maid behind, with a bucket of water, a *boule chaude,* a flask of cognac, a cushion for my back, and a rug for my knees — in fact, "all the comforts of home." But she knows that I would much prefer to be killed outright than suffocated in a *cave.*

As I had anything but a comfortable time at home the night before I left, I really could not see what difference it made where I was. One side of the *tir de barrage* seemed to me as good as the other, though I will confess that I prefer to listen out of doors, in the air, than shut up in a room, even when honours are easy as to danger.

The last words Amélie said to me were "I do hope the Gothas won't go to Paris with you this time." But they did.

However I had a good night Saturday, and passed a quiet Sunday, resting in a cosy room, free from any responsibility, and talking about anything that was not war, and I enjoyed it. But I paid up for it that night, when, just as I was getting into bed, that abominable *sirène* went wailing through the street, and almost at the same moment the bombs began to fall. This was even before we heard the barrage, and then, for three long hours and more, the cannon boomed, the machine guns spat, and the bombs exploded. It was a simply infernal racket.

If you want an example of how some of the simple people take it, here is one. The *bonne* in the house where I visit is a girl from Nimes, who used to live in a convent. Needless to say that she is very religious. She has no sense of fear. Perhaps she does not know enough to be afraid, — maybe I wrong her. She sleeps in the top of the house. The only thing she, who loves her bed, hates, is being waked up. Her orders are to come downstairs, when the *alerte* begins. But she rarely does. On that night, for some reason, possibly because there was a bad fire, she came down. The house was chilly, so she was told to lie on the sofa in the dining-room. She obeyed, and fell asleep at once, and peacefully slept right through it all.

When it was over I went to the door and called her, told her that it was over, and that she could go up to bed.

She rose, sleepily, looking a bit dazed, and then said: "Is it over, Madame?" Then she piously blessed herself, and in a hurried voice, just as you have heard people murmur their prayers *sotto voce,* she added, "God pity those less lucky than we have been," and went back to bed. I am positive that she was asleep in five minutes, and as I already know those who claim to have slept through raids it may be possible that I am wrong about people not becoming accustomed to them, and that, if they go on frequently, we may all sleep right through.

I suppose that you know that the government conceals, as far as possible, all the damage done by these air raids. The newspapers give no details. The part of the city damaged is never mentioned. The official announcement contains merely the fact that the raid began at a certain hour, that there was or was not material damage done, when it ended, and whether or not there were victims. Of course the people in the vicinity hit by the bombs know, and the muzzled newspapers know, but you would be surprised at the small excitement there is. The object of the silence is, of course, to conceal from Germany the result of these raids. I've my doubts if that is possible. It seems to me that nothing can be concealed from them. I'm not sure that, in some diabolical way, they don't know what I am writing to you this very minute. But if the reticence does not achieve that object, it proves very effective in circumscribing excitement, which, under the old reporting methods, would have been inevitable, and the effects of the raid do not become the one topic of the day's conversation in the streets. This raid was an especially disastrous one, as there was a fire in an important part of the city. Yet it was only by the merest accident that, forty-eight hours later, I passed through the famous quarter which was most damaged, and although it was wonderfully cleaned up, — the fire department goes to work at once, — and even daylight which follows the raid finds many traces removed — it seemed to me that for half a mile on both sides of the Boulevard St. Germain, where it runs between the government buildings, there was not a whole pane of glass — yet there was no irreparable harm done, and the loss of life was not heavy.

Amélie met me at the station when I came home, in a very nervous frame of mind. She literally yanked me out of the train, and said emphatically: "Well, thank God, here you are. You are not going to Paris again until these raids are over. It makes us all too nervous. You are better off at home."

When I got up the hill and saw what had happened here I did not blame her for being nervous, although I confess that I could not see that one place was any improvement on the other. Thirty bombs and a torpedo or two had been sprinkled along the valley from Vaires to Crécy-en-Brie. A big bomb fell in the field on the other side of the *route nationale,* and made a hole fifteen yards square and nine yards deep. Five bombs fell on Bouleurs, and a torpedo, which did not explode, fell the other side of Quincy in what is called the "*terre noire*." The bomb which fell near the château shook the whole hill, and it was quite evident that it had shaken Amélie's nerves, and that she had not recovered.

The result is that there is a general fit of trembling everywhere, and it is the fashion here to sleep in the caves. There is a machine gun set up at the Demi-Lune, the water-mains on the top of the hill — the Paris water from the Ourcq passes there — have been examined, as have our local mains, — Couilly has running water — and hose attached. The firemen, of whom I have never heard before, have materialized. All this active preparation for a local defence ought to calm the people, but, of course, it does not. It only emphasizes the fact that it is necessary, and to them, waiting so long in suspense for the beginning of a spring action, seems to presage hard days.

There have always been rigid rules about lights here from the first air raids, so long ago. They have been forgotten, with the result that thirty people were fined to-day for uncovered lights, and the rules are made more rigid than ever. I have been notified that my shutters are not sufficient, and have to hustle to get some sort of heavy inside curtains for a house which at this moment seems all doors and windows. The truth is, the part of my house where the lights show is the guest chamber, never used except when the soldiers are here, as they are now.

All circulation in the roads after dark is forbidden. Wagons cannot carry lights, nor foot-passenger lanterns. It has been the habit for people from Couilly to come running up the hill, lantern in hand, to watch the raids on Paris from here, and there is a theory that it was these lanterns on the road which drew the bombs on the hill Sunday. It may be, but as there was a big *cantonnement* of troops here that seems a better explanation, while it is not unlikely that some of the Gothas which failed to get through the *barrage,* not wishing to return to their base, carrying their bombs with them, may simply have dropped them any old place. All these things are guesses, of course.

The weather is lovely. I am getting a lot of work done in my garden—among other things, sand laid in all the paths,—after trying for four years. The *poilus* did it for me. It will make life much easier, as I can walk in the garden in winter. It will also be a comfort to Amélie, as I shall not track in the mud, and neither will Khaki and Dick.

XX

March 28, 1918

CAN it be less than a fortnight ago that I wrote to you? My letter-book says so, but it is hard to believe. I seem to have lived a century since.

The cables have told you the mere facts, of course. You know that the long-expected offensive presaged by the concentration of the German hordes from the Russian frontier began on the 21st, when they were flung against our lines, from Cherizy in the north to Panisiaux Bois in the south, and that, in six days, the Allies have lost all their hard-earned advances of three years. In six days all the sacrifices of three years have been rendered vain, and last night our line was sixty miles, in some places, west of where it had been on the morning of March 21st. In the lost land are the scenes of so much hard fighting, land over which the Allies had crept inch by inch — all lost in six days, — Peronne, Bapaume, Ham, Roye, Noyon and oh! how many tragic hilltops, and how many spots where our beloved dead lie buried!

But even though you read these things, you have no idea of what the week has meant to us living so near it, to us, who, day after day, have followed the brave boys in the advance, and felt, as they felt, that no inch of ground gained *could* be lost again.

The hours of those first days will always be unforgettable hours of tragedy. I have many times written of the dread we have felt of some such thing ever since the Germans were in a position to remove their defensive army from the east. But never, in my greatest anxiety, did I dream of this.

March 21st was a beautiful Thursday.

Louise and I were working in the garden. I was setting out pansies in the bed under the elderberry bushes, on the side of the hill.

It was during the morning that I began to hear far-off guns, but I took little notice, until after noon, when the booming became so heavy that the very ground in which I had my hands seemed to tremble under me — or was it my hands that were trembling? I don't know.

It lasted all day, and the guns were still thundering when I went out on the lawn before going up to bed, — to look off to the north.

At intervals I heard it all night, and once, in the night, I went out to look, and could see the lights in the sky, and now and then a rocket. I heard the voices of Père and Amélie, and knew that they were hanging out of their window, watching the north also.

I cannot tell you what the sleepless suspense, and the waiting for the morning was like. I was still in bed, waiting for Amélie to arrive on the morning of the 22nd, when I heard some one running along the terrace, and a voice called: "*Vous êtes éveillée, Madame?*"

I went to the window.

There stood my next-door neighbour, white as a sheet.

"Oh, Madame," she cried, "the Germans have attacked our line on a front of ninety kilometres. We are retreating on the whole line. My God, my God!" And she went on down the hill to carry the news to Voisins.

Even while I was standing, stupefied, I heard the drums beating the *assemblage générale* in Voisins, for the 89th Infantry are still with us.

By the time I was dressed the boys were coming in relays to say "good-bye," and to announce that the *camions* were coming at eleven.

The morning was a repetition of that of last spring, when the 118th advanced to Soissons.

It was impossible to work. No one could. It was just after noon that the *camions* began to arrive.

As the trees are not yet leaved out, I could see, from the lawn, the long line of grey *camions* drawn up at equal spaces from each other all along the *route* to Meaux, and, at intervals, the soldiers, *sac au dos,* standing in groups ready to mount to their places.

It was two o'clock when they began to move, and from that time, night and day, until Sunday morning of the 24th, the line of advancing troops, cannon, artillery, field-kitchens, — was absolutely unbroken. They occupied all the roads about us, even that on the canal. Along the *route nationale* and the *route du canal* of Meaux they moved, rumbling at top speed, about ten yards apart, and along the *route* towards Esbly, through Condé, wound all the horse-drawn vehicles and the cavalry. Overhead hummed the aeroplanes, keeping watch.

Every day the news that came was bad. Every day the Allies were being driven back, and last night they were within twelve miles of Amiens, already evacuated.

To make the whole situation sadder, by Sunday night, the refugees, driven for the second time from their homes, began to pass through over all our *routes*. That is what brings panic. It would carry it as far as Paris, if Paris had to see it, but in the city the movement is concentrated about the Gare du Nord, and the Gare de l'Est, and there the organization is wonderful. In the entire evacuation I am told that the American boys are doing heroic work.

All the week I have fought against panic

here. Faith, you understand, I am sure, had received a hard blow. Fear seemed suddenly to have taken root everywhere, a thing I have never seen here before,— fear that the Germans were too strong in numbers still, and the Americans not only unprepared, but not yet numerous enough to turn the balance, for in the first few days before Amiens the Allies fought, at times, one to six, and some say, at an even greater disadvantage.

To make the situation all the harder for the civilians — for they had to get hold of their nerves, and they did it,— the Germans threw all their resources against us at once, not only at the front against the armies, but against the civilians in the rear; it was the very exaggeration of their warfare of terror.

On Saturday morning, the third day of the battle, — at about half-past seven — as I was sitting in the garden listening to the guns, I heard an explosion in the direction of Paris, and, while I was wondering what it could mean, the church bells all along the valley began to ring out an *alerte*. I had not heard a sound even resembling a *moteur* in the air and the sound from Paris was not in the least like that made familiar by the air raids. Besides, the Germans have never attempted an air raid by daylight, although the English have. It could not have been more than a half hour later that there was another sound exactly like the first in the same direction. But this time there was no *alerte,* and there was no noise of the guns for the defence of the city against *avions.* At regular intervals all day, while we read the trying news from the front,—eighty divisions of German soldiers thrown against the British—we heard that sound from Paris repeated.

About half-past four in the afternoon Amélie's nephew, a lad of sixteen, who works in an ammunition place, arrived from Paris—his train over an hour and a half late—with the news that Paris was being bombarded from the air—that the attack began a little after seven—that there had been no *alerte* until after the bombardment began, and, that up to the time he left, no German *avions* had been heard by the listening posts anywhere, and yet once in about fifteen minutes a bomb fell.

That was all very mysterious.

I asked him if much damage had been done, and if there was any panic.

He said he had heard that several people had been killed, but there was no panic. When the *sirènes* went through the streets after the first bomb, people ran, as usual, for the *abris,* but as silence followed they gradually came out into the streets, and stood about, gazing up into the air. No sign of any air machine—any *Boche*—had been seen. When the lad left Paris there was a spirit of curiosity rather than alarm, and the only harm he had actually seen was a newspaper kiosk, near the railway station, destroyed, and a hole in the ground. That looked serious enough, considering the situation. But "a miss is as good as a mile."

The next day, Sunday—a day too beautiful to look on such horrid deeds—we got the explanation. It seemed inconceivable, but it is evidently true. The latest war exploit of the Huns is a gun set up—so the aviators say—somewhere near La Fère, where the Yorkshire boys fought their last battle before retreating here in September, 1914,—a gun which is bombarding Paris at a distance variously stated at from sixty-five to eighty miles,—either distance seems equally incredible, but it is evidently true. The military authorities are said to have it placed. The question is to destroy it. But you probably heard all about this by cable.

The son of one of my neighbours who is at home on leave—he is an aviator to-day; he was a farmer in 1914,—said, as we were listening to this gun yesterday, for it is still at work:

"Madame, this is war. If we want to win, we have got to get rid of all our civilian ideas. If nations do not want to put up with things of this sort, why they must find another way than war to settle their disputes. No one would be in the least sentimental about killing a tiger and its whelps. Why pretend to a finer feeling about an enemy more dangerous than a tiger — an enemy so dangerous that even when we get him down — and we shall — I don't see how the world can go on unless we exterminate him, even if it takes this generation. If we, stupidly, do not, then we must suffer for it later. Be sure of one thing, if the *Boches* get us down, they 'll wipe *us* out. The whole earth is not big enough for both of us."

Anyway, there is a point of view for you.

On the fourth day of the bombardment of Paris, while every one was divided between anxiety about the battle in the north and pride at the superb spirit of desperate resistance of our armies, I got a letter from Paris which gave us all a good laugh — for I translated for Amélie, knowing that she would tell it everywhere — and better it in the telling. It spoke of the splendid spirit of the bombarded capital, which had already returned to normal life — tramways running, street-life calm, school-children in the radius of the bombardment being taken out of danger; and it told of the first effort to announce the beginning of the daily bombardment by an *alerte* to be given by the city police, who were ordered to beat a drum in the streets — a sort of city revival of our country town crier. The Sergent de Ville, who has his *amour propre,* protested. He did not know how to drum,—drumming is a *métier* like any other. The city replied, "Never mind that. Put the drum on. Take these two sticks, and go along pounding. We've no time to give you lessons. Every one will know what it means."

They were properly humiliated, but they had to obey. Away they had to go, beating their drums, and beside them marched the *gamins* of Paris, pounding on tin cans, and whatever would make a noise. Of course all Paris roared with laughter. The blushing Sergents de Ville returned to their posts, and they never went out any more as drummers. Isn't that deliciously Paris? Too bad Mr. Hohenzollern could not have seen it.

But though this made a short diversion here we did not laugh long. Yesterday it looked dangerously like a panic again. For a few hours it seemed as if all our efforts could not prevent people here from evacuating the place,—without orders. If the news had not been better this morning I hate to think what might have happened.

Last night we heard no guns. This morning's *communiqué* announced that the German advance has been practically stopped—at all events the Allies are holding them—the breaches in the line have been filled—it is unbroken—*but* after a retreat of nearly sixty miles, and all they have worked for and won inch by inch, lost from Noyon north, except a bit of Flanders.

It is a sin to look back, I know. Our road lies in the future. I hope no one over there whom I love will ever have to fight depression as I have fought it since a week ago to-day. I suppose the turn of you across the water is coming. Still, you will never have to see poor women and little children flying from their homes, as we see them every day. They never complain. They are grateful for the slightest sympathy. They invariably tell you of cases they know of people so much worse off than they are.

I hope you are not worrying about me. I could not write you all these details if I did not know — was not sure — that long before you read it, the situation will be changed for the better, that the cable will have reassured you, so that all this will only be *interesting* to you, who want to know always the truth about my life.

They tell us at the *Mairie* that, while the *Boches* may advance a little at one point or another in the line, the push is absolutely over, and that it has been out of all proportion costly for the Germans. With that we have to be content. We must wait for history to tell us of the glorious episodes of the desperate battles, of the achievements of the cavalry which closed the breaches in the line, and how the French 5th Army Corps — our brave boys of the Seine and Marne — held the road down the valley of the Oise to the beating heart of France — Paris — for the second time. How long?

XXI

April 15, 1918

We are droll, we humans.

Although the battle is still going on out there every one here seems to have forgotten those panicky hours of the last week in March. It was that first quick retreat in the north which upset them all with the unspeakable dread that perhaps we could not hold them. The moment when it became evident that, though the Allies had to retreat, the line was not smashed, every one bucked up — and life became just what it had been all these forty-two and a half months before. People seem even to have forgotten the dread of those days.

The second phase of the battle was over a week ago, and, though we have lost some ground, the line is still an unbroken wall, and Germany's situation unchanged — except that she is a little nearer Paris.

We 've had some queer weather — most uncertain. It has rained, sunshined, snowed, sunshined and frozen. I am afraid that means another year without fruit, which is a disappointment, as the fruit trees flowered superbly.

The long-distance cannon continues to fire on Paris — the *grosse Bertha,* they call it. We hear every shot from here. The cannon at the front still pounds away, and during the nights the battle-front is often strangely illuminated, a dull glow, like that which I am sure you have often seen in the sky over a foundry, and not unlike that which, at times, hangs over Vesuvius. Now and then we see star rockets and different kinds of *fusées.* But I no longer go out at night to watch, though I cannot induce Père and Amélie to sleep. The truth is that I have got so that the cannon do not keep me awake. Amélie insists that she cannot sleep, but as her room is on the south side of the house, I believe that is only because she persists in getting up and hanging out of the north window to see what is going on, thus deliberately preventing herself from sleeping.

I keep myself very busy. It is the only way. I go up to Paris whenever there is any need, much to Amélie's disgust. She never draws a long breath, she says, until I get back, on the theory that a bomb from that long-range gun will fall on the train one day, or on me in the street. But as the chances are about one in a million I 'll take that chance. I was in Paris three times last week — going up twice by the seven o'clock train, and coming back at night. Of course, only important business would have induced me to make that effort, as it meant taking my coffee at half-past five, and I don't like that any better than I ever did.

In spite of everything I had heard, I found Paris normal. It is a very great pity that the Germans, who are told that Paris is being bombarded every day, and probably suppose it is being gradually destroyed, cannot see the effects of the bombardment. I was on the boulevards the first day I went up, when a bomb fell and exploded, making so heavy a detonation that it seemed very near. It really was across the Seine. No one stopped walking, though every one did exactly what I did—pulled out a watch to see the hour. That was all, though it was only a short time after the Good Friday feat of the *grosse Bertha,* when a bomb fell on the church you and I know so well, and where we used to go in the old days, and sitting near the tomb of Madame de Maintenon's ribald first husband—chair-bound old Scarron—listen to the very service that was going on when the bomb fell. What with the bomb, and the panic that followed, there was heavy loss of life, and because of the number of victims, and the fact that many were well-known people,—for the Good Friday office of the Tenebrae is a smart religious function,—the accident made a good deal of noise in the world, and it was impossible to conceal it. But it is ridiculous to emphasize the fact that the dirty Germans deliberately fired on a church on a Holy Day during an office, as the reaching of such a target was pure accident. The emplacement of the big gun is fixed. It reaches a certain distance into the city. It can evidently be turned east and west, so that the menaced points seem to lie in an arc, reaching roughly from Montrouge to near the Gare de l'Est, and passing by a line just behind where I used to live — through the "Garden of Lies," I imagine, — and across the Seine near the Louvre.

Twice while I was in Paris I had to pass through this line, while the gun was firing, to go out through the fortifications. I was on my way to a suburban hospital, and had a sick woman in the motor-car. The big gun fired a corking shot while we were crossing the Seine to run up by the Luxembourg Gardens. I looked at my watch and calculated the distance to the Porte, but I had not the smallest sensation of the suspense I expected to have. Three hours later I came back by the same route, only making a slight detour to avoid a tree that a shot fired since I passed out of the gate had broken off.

The only marked difference that I saw in the quarter was the silence in the Luxembourg Gardens, where the children were no longer playing. Apropos of the children, you might suppose that living in a bombarded city, being in so many cases taken out of bed and carried to *abris* in the night, might at least create a panic among them. It does not seem to. On the contrary many of them appear to think it all a lark.

In the danger zone, of course, Paris, which takes great care of her children — for nowhere are children more loved or happier than they are in France — has sent the school-children, with their teachers, into the country. But there are still plenty of children in the city.

One day when I was in town I saw a group of youngsters playing and making so much noise that I had to stop and watch them. It was in a garden in a safe part of the city, and it took two minutes to see what they were playing. They were playing "*Les Gothas*." One boy was a watcher at a "listening post," who gave the alarm, "They come!" Another was the fireman in his auto, rushing along, and sounding his *sirène*. One was the gunner at his post of D. C. A. putting up a *barrage*, "bang, bang, bang." A group were Boche *avions* making a terrible series of explosions in all parts of the garden. When it was over, the bogus dead and wounded were lying all over the place, and a tiny little fellow rushed about, sounding the "All clear," on a tin trumpet. Even then it was not over, for along came the clanging bells of the ambulances and the victims were picked up. They did the thing with great spirit, imitating all the noises admirably, with children's apt talent at mimicry.

I never go to Paris but I wish that you were with me. Each trip into the city has its new experience.

The railway station is one of the most interesting places in the world to-day. Our line carries most of the soldiers going to and from the front.

At Vaires, just outside of the outer line of forts, is the immense *Camp des Permissionaires.* All the men coming in from the front on their regular eight days' home-leave once in four months, must stop at Vaires to have their papers examined, and from there go on to their destinations, and many of them stay there during their leave, for obvious reasons. At the expiration of their leave, they report there to be sent back to their posts. The camp is immense. Line after line of tracks has been laid, extending almost as far as one can see, for the big military trains run right into the camp from the main line. Miles and miles of barracks, and offices for re-equipping soldiers, stretch off into the distance, and there is never an hour of the day or night, when a train-load of *poilus* is not coming in or going out.

As this is only a short distance down the line between here and Paris it is one of the most interesting points on my trips to town.

The big station in Paris, with its various Red Cross works,—the Americans have a very well-organized one there—and moving throngs, is even more interesting. It is alive with movement—with tragedy and comedy—and to-day it is a tower of Babel, with the American military policeman in his red bands and his conspicuous U. S. A. always in evidence.

I never can resist lingering a minute to see the soldiers leaving the station. There are always crowds of women and children waiting at the barriers—for the *poilus* have their especial entrance and exit—and a throng always presses round the gate through which they must pass, not only those who have come expecting—usually in vain—to meet their own,—but the curious who have just come to see the boys from the front. The looker after material—artistic, realistic, or otherwise,—lovers of the grotesque, hunters after the picturesque, lovers of laughter, morbid seekers after tragedy, will find it all there, as well as, now and then, something of the beautiful, and occasionally a bit of the heroic. But the seeker after what is ordinarily known as "scenes" will lose his time. France may have once been what we used to call her, "hysterical." She is certainly not even emotional to-day, so far as I can see.

Sometimes I think that the big station is

even more picturesque on the side where the *poilus* are waiting to go back. At those times the big courtyard in front is packed with them. When they are coming in from the front, they simply seem to rush through, taking little notice of the crowd so interested in them and providing the atmosphere involuntarily. But when they are going back to the front it is a different matter.

Do you find that puzzling? Well, the *poilus* arriving on home-leave are tired, often disgusted, or indifferent. "Home-leave" looks like Heaven to them. But they go back gaily. The truth is, as a rule, they are glad to go back. It is not that they are not tired of the war. They are. Every one is, — except our boys, who are nearly four years behind the game. It has lasted too long for the *poilu* to have anything but dogged tolerance for it. When the regular time arrives for him to "come out" he welcomes it, *but* in the three and more years that he has been cut off from normal life he has become the inhabitant of another world. He speaks another language — a specialized tongue, — and, in spite of everything, he almost invariably gets homesick on leave.

I suspected this, little by little, as I watched the men coming in from the front — they are no longer boisterous, — and then watched them go singing back. So one day I said to Petit Louis, a boy in our *commune*, a gunner, who always comes to pay his respects to me when he arrives on leave, and to say "good-bye" when "going in" again.

"Well, Louis, how is your *soixante-quinze?*"

"Fine, the darling," he laughed.

Then I said that I supposed he was glad to be at home.

He puckered up his brows, shrugged his shoulders, made one of his queer little gestures with his hands, and said:

"Well, I don't know. Sure, I am glad to see the woman and the kids, and to sleep one night or so in a bed,—but—I don't know why it is, I get bored with it in a day or two. I am used to a different kind of life. I miss my chums. I miss knowing exactly what to do—what I 've got to do whether I want to or not. So you see, after two days of walking about, talking with people who seem to understand just nothing at all about what is going on out there, I am bored. I miss being dead tired at night. I miss the noise. After two or three days I count the hours until I can get back."

I can understand that. It made me think of what a man said to me in Paris in the early days of the war.

"My father used to go, once a year, to sit over a dinner with his comrades of the regiment in '70. My sons will cherish their comrades and live over with them this great war.

Men of my generation—we have nothing to talk about."

It was not worth while to remind him that after this is over the men who will be heard talking loudest will be those who have never seen a trench or fired a gun. Here in our little *commune* the people who can tell you the wildest tales of the days of the invasion are those who ran away. If anyone were to come here to-day, in a spirit of research, it would not be the half dozen of us who actually stayed here in September, 1914, who would tell hair-raising tales. It would be the others. The stories have rolled up like the famous snowball. It has opened my eyes in a sense about the difficulties of writing history.

One of the striking features about this war is that the active soldiers almost never talk with the civilians about the war. In a sense, it is forbidden, but the reason goes deeper than that. The soldier and the civilian seem to-day to speak a different language. It almost seems as if a dark curtain hung between the realities of life "out there," and the life into which the soldier enters *en repos*.

Whenever they are talkative, it is of something rather spiritual than material. The last time I went up to Paris I had an experience of that sort. I was settled in my compartment—alone. The train was about to start when the door was yanked open. A tall, middle-aged officer brought up his hand to salute, flung his bag in, entered after it, banged the door, and sat down just as the train moved. He cast a keen glance at me, then unbuckled his belt and made himself comfortable. The first time he caught my eyes he leaned over, and said:

"I imagine that you are the American lady who lived up on the hill at Huiry?"

I owned up.

"I have heard of you," he said. "I have a friend who was quartered in your house."

Then he settled down to chat. He seemed to need it, which is unusual. He appeared to be about forty-five, — a lieutenant. He asked all sorts of things about the States — how long it would take their army to get ready? What sort of soldiers did I think they would make? How many did I think were over? And so forth.

I did my best, but I could not tell him how many were over, and we would not be really ready until the army was here. The only thing of which I could actually assure him was that the boys from the States would, with a little experience, make as fine soldiers as the war has yet seen. On that point I was absolutely sure, and I gave it to him, with emphasis, that, in my opinion, old Kaiser Bill would have no greater disillusion in the war than the United States would furnish him, in proving to him that it did not take a lifetime of drilling to create a patriotic army, and that a patriotic army was better than a professional one.

With a sigh of content he leaned back, and I realized again how great a factor in the *morale* of the French the coming over of the boys from the States was. After a short silence he smiled at me, and said:

"Ridiculous — a war. You see, in the days before this came I was what one calls, with considerable contempt now, 'an intellectual.' I did not believe in force. I believed in the spiritual development of the individual. But in days of peace does any man know what is really in him? I 've given my only son," and he touched the black band on his sleeve. "Thank God his mother went first. I 've done my duty as best I could," and he touched the red ribbon on his breast, with the barred one of military medals beside it. "But I often wonder if all educated men have to make the same struggle that I do. Often, when the moment comes to 'go over' I wonder what my men would think if I were to cry out, 'Fire in the air! It is nobler to be killed than to kill.'" He looked out of the window a moment before he laughed and added, "Absurd, is n't it? Because I know that a war of defence and for principle, and for the hopes of the future, is a holy war."

Here the train began to slow down.

"Helloa! Vaires already? I hope that I have not bored you?" And as he buckled his belt, and picked up his bag, he added, "It is so rarely that I talk to a woman — I've no family — that I rather lose my head. A thousand excuses. Good-bye." And we shook hands like old friends.

I watched him as he walked rapidly away. A lieutenant at forty-five! That meant that he was a volunteer.

I have been sitting here, off and on, all day, writing this. That shows my need of communion in these trying days, when we are asking ourselves where the next attack is to be, and hoping that it will not take us by surprise.

I smile when I remember that in the first hard days of the first week in March I tried to comfort the people about me by saying: "Courage! This is the beginning of the final act." So it is, I suppose. But there are to be more scenes in it than I thought then. They are still strong, those Huns.

I do hope that when I write so frankly of the emotions of each day here you do not get the impression that anyone has lost faith in the final issue. I don't think they have. It is only that they are not so sure as they were up to the opening of this offensive that this special part of France may not have to be sacrificed as so many places have been. If it is — well, never mind. In our hearts, even trembling, we instinctively believe in a second miracle. Yet why should we?

XXII

May 24, 1918

WE are still sitting as tight as we can, waiting for the next offensive move, which has held off longer than was anticipated. The absolute uncertainty as to the point in the line now menaced, and the inevitable nervousness which comes from waiting every night for an aerial attack, and listening all day for the big cannon to begin firing on Paris, makes each hour of the twenty-four a bit trying. Of course the last of the three *grosse Berthas* was destroyed by the aviators on the 3rd. But we know that it will not stay out of action forever.

I have kept busy planting, cleaning house, arranging all sorts of extra curtains, but, luckily the nights are getting very short and the Gotha raids do not force me to be hermetically sealed for long at a time. It is hardly dark at half-past nine, and it begins to get light before four. I have already learned to go about in my shuttered house in the dark when an *alerte* gets me out of bed, though there is no need. But an odd sensation comes over me during an attack, especially as the batteries for the defence surround us now in a semicircle — there are five of them. When they all begin to fire, I feel as if my little house were the only visible thing in the landscape, and as though, if I lit up, even behind shutters and curtains, I should be seen. If that is not the *n*th power of vanity, I don't know what to name it.

I expect you will get tired of hearing about air raids, but really, if I do not tell you about them I should be at a loss to know of what I could write to you. They are of almost nightly occurrence, and each one is different. We had a double one last night, — or one in two acts — covering four hours and a half, with an *entr'acte* of three quarters of an hour.

It was about eleven o'clock. I was reading quietly when I heard the guns from the fort. I intended to stay comfortably in bed. It had been understood between Amélie and me that, under no circumstances, was she to come to me. In the first place, it is forbidden by orders, and in the second, now that the *barrage* surrounds us, there is danger from spent shot from the guns of the forts. But at the end of half an hour I could not resist going out to try to see what was happening. I had hardly got into the garden before the guns ceased firing, and I went back to bed. It was only a little over an hour later, when *boom* went the cannon again, and the raid lasted until nearly daylight. This time I went out at once. It is impossible to resist the impulse. In spite of all the regulations there was a group in the road above my house, at a point where they can look right over the fort at Chelles into the horizon line over Paris, and from which point they can see and locate each searchlight and can often see the explosion of the shells. I suppose they will continue to do this until a bit of spent shrapnel hits some one in the head, and demonstrates to them that it is not safe.

It made a rather long night, but when the last gun fired, just before daybreak, I was still sitting on the lawn. All through the night I had heard the military trains on the railroad rushing along the valley, and, when the dim coming of day enabled me to see them, I noticed that a scouting engine preceded each train, as in the early days of the mobilization. So I was not surprised a few hours later to learn that a bomb had fallen within fifty yards of the tunnel at Charlifert.

While I was still sitting there, Amélie joined me. She was all dressed, and I knew that she had not been in bed at all.

It was not quite four o'clock. A beautiful day was breaking. The cuckoo was talking. A blackbird began to sing. Then the sparrows and the swallows yawned and chirped, and a thrush piped up. Overhead, the *avions de chasse* were still scouting. Out at the big camp, lying along miles of the fields, across the Marne, *flèchettes,* thin white lines of light, mounted like silver arrows straight into the air at regular intervals, to guide the aviators back to their landing field. Now and then, a coloured light in the air announced a flyer ready to descend, then, in a moment, the big lights on the field would flare up, and in the coming daylight we would see a machine circling down. We sat there, until, at half-past four, the last homing *avion* was in. It was no use to go to bed at that hour, so, as the days are hot, I weeded and watered the garden, set out a few begonias which Amélie went to Meaux for yesterday, and some of the seedlings — zinnias, soucis, and old-fashioned balsam. I promise myself to go to bed with the chickens to-night to make up.

I note that you send your love to Khaki and Dick. I have given your message to the Grand Duc, but Dick is very unpopular at this moment, and civilities are suspended between us.

I think I told you that Dick had got so that he never barked at a *poilu?* The army might come and carry off the house, and me in it, he would consider it all right. Like the *Grande' Duchesse* he loves the military. Well, lately, life has been very dull for him. Since he cannot run free without a muzzle, his one idea is to escape, and go in search of his adored *poilus,* since they don't just now come to see him. I expect they let him lick out their *gamelles.* It saves washing them. Anyway, last week there was a regiment at Quincy. Dick disappeared. He was gone for nearly a week. I kept hearing of him, but the regiment had been gone nearly forty-eight hours before he reappeared. Amélie opened the door for him. He made a dash upstairs and tried to jump on the bed to give me an affectionate morning greeting, as he is allowed to do when he is good. I repulsed him severely, and tried to have an explanation with him. I demanded, at least, to know where he had been since the regiment departed. He was very reticent. He looked at me, and scratched his head behind his ear in a very knowing manner — had brought a military flea with him, I suppose, — and expected that to satisfy me. It distinctly did not. So he was sent down to his kennel and chained. I hope he knew why. Still, as he had evidently had a good time, he probably felt that it was worth while being chained up for a day.

However, the explanation I could not get from him followed almost at once. He had evidently waited about in Quincy hoping some more soldiers might arrive, and in the waiting time he had been overcome by hunger, and gone marketing for himself — on tick, — and his bills followed him home.

He had eaten a franc-twenty-five centimes' worth of sausage at the *charcuterie*. He had spoiled a pound of cheese at the *crémerie*. He had decamped with a bone worth fifty centimes at the butcher's, which would have been allowed him if he had not returned and helped himself to a costly chop — one franc-fifty. On the morning of the third day, — no regiment arriving, — he evidently decided that life was too difficult, and that he had better return to his regular boarding-house, where, at least, meals were certain, and wait until more soldiers and more *gamelles* arrived. I paid the bills of the prodigal, of course, but I did not kill any fatted calf for him. Not that he minded that, for, to tell you the truth, he rendered up some of the stolen goods soon after his return, and then rolled himself up to sleep it off.

While I am speaking about Dick, I must tell you another amusing thing. He has discovered the aeroplanes. For a long time, whenever a machine flew low, as they often do, he has rushed out and barked furiously all over the place. Just for fun, one day, I held him by his collar and tried to make him look in the right direction. I never succeeded. He looked everywhere but at the proper place over his head. But one day, standing with Amélie and me in the garden while a big triplane was passing, he discovered it himself. He began barking, running madly after it, and trying to jump the hedge. Since then, he has learned where to look when he hears them, and he always runs the length of the garden, eyes in the air, head erect, yelping and jumping. Of course, he thinks it is a big bird, though he never barks at birds. But birds don't make such a racket.

I have seen some wonderful flights of *avions* lately — some twenty in battle formation. It is a wonderful sight here where the sky space is so extensive. One of the prettiest flights the other day was so high that, if it had not been for the noise the *moteurs* made, I should not have detected them at all, — they looked so tiny in the blue depth of that vast expanse — no larger than the swallow flying under them, thousands and thousands of feet below.

Kind of you to congratulate me on dropping out of the political note. As for that, I was stirred when Caillaux went to live at *La Santé,* and I shall get excited again when he — goes on. For all the smaller men who are moving out of the line of vision I am little concerned so that they go and *en route* close the pincers on the chief. Political trials are delicate affairs in the democratic world in which a man is said to have a right to his opinions, but in times of war there are things more important than opinions. The discipline to which an army defending the country must submit, and failure to do which incurs the penalty of death for the soldier, surely applies in some way to civilians. Until it is demonstrated that it does, there can be no consolations for the terrible affair of last May, or for the tragedy of Coeuvres. That is all.

XXIII

May 30, 1918

It has been a very trying week. Indeed, as I look back to the long months of war, I realize that it was only when, on the last day of January, Germany began the effort of which this week is only one phase, that we really began to appreciate the frightfulness of her endeavour. Since that day, no one within hearing of the front has had a day of tranquillity, and no one in France an hour free of anxiety. For that matter, no one in the world, capable of understanding or sympathy, can have been calm. But it is surely a different thing to read about these days than to take part in them. I cannot write you about the life here in detail, because, as I have already assured you, things are all changed by the time you read the letters, and you know long before you get them what turn affairs have taken. And then, there is always the censor.

There has hardly been a night since I wrote you last without an air raid, and on the night of the day I last wrote you, we were showered with spent shrapnel. It fell on the roofs at Voisins and I am treasuring for you, as a personal souvenir of me and the war, a large jagged bit which struck the shutter of my bedroom window and bounded on to the terrace.

On the day before the long-awaited offensive began on our front, on the historic Chemin des Dames, everything was quiet here. It was a Sunday. We had had five air raids in about eight days. The weather had been very hot, and I had felt a bit shaky. But on Saturday, that was the twenty-fifth, I had a telegram from Paris telling me that a friend was leaving for Bordeaux on Monday, and, as she could not get a *sauf conduit* to come to me, begged me to come up to town, if only for an hour. So I was up at five, and at six Père was driving me down to the station to take the seven o'clock train. We always have to allow plenty of time for fear of being delayed on the road by military *camions*.

It was a lovely morning, full of sunshine, but with the fresh breeze blowing from the north-east still, as it has for weeks. As we turned from the Chemin Madame into the *route nationale,* we found ourselves face to face with a procession of artillery *camions* extending as far as we could see in the direction of Meaux, and down the hill to Couilly, where, one after another, they continued to come round the curve from St. Germain during our entire descent to the station. The *camions* had cannon of all calibres mounted, each followed by a load of gunners, and every little way came ammunition-trucks and rolling kitchens. Every cannon's nose, as it stuck its carefully capped muzzle between the heads of the chauffeur and mechanician was wreathed with flowers, and every *camion* carried a huge bunch of red peonies or roses, with daisies and some blue field flowers — always making the French colours. The gunners all had clean, smiling, Sunday faces, but, as Ninette ambled down the hill in the cloud of dust made by the *camions* groaning and rumbling up it, I felt that this tremendous movement of artillery must be the prelude to the offensive, and that the movement just here must mean that it was the line from Soissons to Reims which was threatened. I said nothing to Père. I was coming back in the middle of the afternoon.

I made an easy trip to Paris. Although it was Sunday, there was no crowd. Nor was there any unusual movement of troops on the line. I found the streets more animated than usual. It was three weeks since the long-range gun, which had so long bombarded the city, had been silenced. It looked as if a great many people who had left Paris during the March offensive had returned. The animation in the streets was not that of even a year ago, but it was anything but a dead city or a sad city to me. So I forgot all about my impression of the morning, until, as I was driving back by the road from Esbly, in the middle of the afternoon, the picture suddenly returned to me, and I instinctively turned to look across the Marne, and listened for the guns. Not a sound. Perhaps I was mistaken, I thought.

We had a peaceful night. I went out early the next morning. All was silent. But while I was having my coffee there was one heavy shot. I jumped. It was once more that big gun firing on Paris. There was no doubt in my mind — that was the accompaniment, or the prelude, to the new battle. But still we heard no sound of artillery in the direction of the front. The only explanation seemed to us was that the attack was, after all, not here but on a part of the line farther north — perhaps again in Picardy where the attack of March had carried the Germans nearer the sea and nearer still to the railroad communication so important to the British. So you can imagine our surprise when the news came that the attack, which had begun at three o'clock in the morning, was against the line in front of us from Montdidier in the west, with Compiègne and the route to Paris down the Oise valley, Chateau Thierry and the route down the Marne, Reims and Chalons, as objectives.

The big gun, which had begun to bombard

Paris at half-past six in the morning was still firing at half-past six at night, and at half-past ten at night there was an air raid which lasted about an hour and a quarter.

With all one's pluck held tight in both hands, and our *morale* builded up on the same principles that are handed out to the soldiers, you must agree that there is something appalling in this determined, reckless exhibition of brute force. Even although I am not a bit sentimental about this, I must remark that it seems to be stupid. The demonstration does not seriously alarm anyone — it surely demoralizes no one. It must be pretty costly. Besides that, the amount of harm it does is infinitesimal in comparison to the effort. One life sacrificed in that way is one too many, but more lives are lost almost any day by the ordinary accidents of life than by this superman effort of frightfulness. As for the air raids — they get less and less effective, as the air defence is elaborated by actual experience.

Trying as the week has been, it has been absolutely different from that of the big battle of March. We have hardly heard a gun. Dead silence has reigned here, and that silence has been terribly trying. We have known that it was largely an infantry battle, and all the time the wind has blown steadily from the north-east — what Amélie calls "*le vent des Boches*," because it is a wind which brings their gas over. But that is the prevailing wind here at this season, and the Germans have made a great study of meteorology, as a military science. In the drive towards Amiens in March, the heavy guns played a big part, and for days and nights the earth shook with the artillery play even as far south as this. To-day, the fourth of this battle, the silence is almost terrifying. I keep saying to myself, "Will the heavy artillery *never* get to work?"

We have lost Craonne, and the Chemin des Dames, and how many a tragic hilltop? Day after day we trace the battle-line as well as we can, and, as it approaches us, the only consolation is that though it bends and curves and stretches, it does not break. The Germans have again crossed the Aisne and the Vesle, and were last night at Fismes, which the English retook in October, 1914, something like twenty miles nearer to us. Reims is holding out superbly. But for that matter, with its tremendous underground structures, it is practically impregnable. I don't believe it can be taken except by a siege, but the Germans are encircling it and rapidly approaching Chateau-Thierry, which threatens our railroad communications.

It was only last week that I had a letter from you in which you said: "Of course they will attack again. They must or own themselves defeated. But they will not be so strong." Hm! They were 650,000 against 80,000 when this battle began. Of course, that was before our reserves were brought up. I sit trembling for fear of a panic again. I cannot blame these poor people. They are as loyal as possible, but our roads are again crowded with refugees flying from the front. It is a horrid sight.

Wednesday a man rested at my gate. He had been obliged to leave his farm when the surprise attack forced the army back so quickly Sunday that civilians had no time to save anything but their lives. He had left his big modern reaping machines — they had to be destroyed to keep them from falling into German hands. He had left two thousand pounds of beans, requisitioned by the army, — there was no time to move them, and they were not paid for — burned that the enemy might not get them. And he is only one of thousands, and it is inevitable that, after the first excitement, must come the sense of personal loss. I could understand that, for this is the second time he had been driven out.

It was hard to find just the right thing to say — especially as I was safe — so far. No personal sacrifice has been asked of me. So I said finally: "Don't be discouraged *yet*. All these things will be arranged, and your children will have a better world to live in. Besides, the American boys are coming over as fast as they can get here. There are nearly a million here now, I should think."

He shook his head. "Too late," he replied. "What are a million against the three millions the Huns have brought from Russia?"

Well, there you are, and can you blame him?

It was Wednesday that things began to look serious here. On that day the scenes of 1914 began to repeat themselves. The better class began to fly. The humbler farmers and peasants began to hide their belongings. Caves and subterranean passages were again filled with furniture, bedding and household treasures, even clothing. Some of the richer farmers began to drive their cattle south, and some people even wheeled their possessions in wheelbarrows to the quarries at Mareuil, where work had stopped, owing to the bombs that have fallen there.

It was in vain that I argued that there was no immediate danger; that we should get warning if it were necessary to go; that the roads were sufficiently blocked already by those who had been driven out, and by the army, without our adding further to the confusion. The peasants and the farmers would listen, — if you set them the example, you can count on them, but not so well on those who have a place to go to, and money in their pockets to get there. Besides, I really was "talking through my hat," and I thought to myself, "If I am a bad prophet they may mob me, and serve me right for interfering."

In the meantime Amélie sat tight. I had her fixed with my eye,—and she had not forgotten 1914.

Thursday—that was yesterday—was the hardest day. All night the confusion on the road was terrible. Sleep was impossible. On that day, while every one was rushing about hiding things—too busy to do any work in the fields—a group of refugees arrived here. As a rule, we, who are off the main road, see them at Quincy and Voisins, and Couilly, and go out to help them. But just before sunset yesterday one of the children of the hamlet came running to the gate with the news that a group of *émigrés* were crossing the hilltop by the Chemin Madame. Of course if they were taking that road, they were coming here. It leads nowhere else. The first impulse of every one seemed to be to hang back. Refugees here, where every one was so nervous, seemed to them the last straw—especially at the moment when they felt pretty sure that another day or two might see them all refugees themselves. But they are children, these simple people. So when I started hurriedly up the road, without a word, to meet them, they all followed, as I knew they would. I thought of how it must feel to be driven out of one's home, and to enter, at sundown of a hot day, into a little hamlet like this, not knowing what kind of a reception awaited one — was it to be a welcome, or only curious looks from indifferent eyes?

As I reached the corner I met coming across the hill a procession of five loaded farm wagons, drawn by big sturdy farm horses. Beside the train marched a middle-aged man and half a dozen boys. In the wagons rode the women and children, and by them ran a couple of dogs. The man walking at the head of the group, with a heavy stick in his hand, looked about fifty, and was apparently the leader. When I smiled him a welcome, he took off his hat, and then we shook hands ceremoniously, and then the Huiry-ites all followed suit. For a moment I thought it was going to be a real function, and I was about to tell him that I was not the Mayor of Huiry, but a foreigner, when I was spared the trouble. He spotted me at once, and said: "*Vous êtes Américaine, n'est-ce pas?*" So much for my accent. He explained that he knew the accent. He had left a lot of our boys where he had come from, — north of Compiègne.

When I asked him what we could do to make the party comfortable, he explained that he had been told that there was room on the hill to shelter his horses for the night, and that that was all they needed. If we could give the old grandmother and her little grandchild a bed, the rest would camp, and then he added: "We don't want to put any one out. We can pay for everything. But the horses must rest for one night, as we have been on the road since sunrise yesterday."

You should have seen how quickly it was arranged. I took in the grandmother — she was not as old as I am, by the way — and the little child, whose father had been killed, and whose mother is a nurse in a hospital in Paris, and a pretty blonde girl, who proved to be the aunt, and inside half an hour the horses were stabled, the wagons under cover, and beds ready for every one, and a kitchen found in the house across the road from me, which was empty.

You can get some idea of what these people are like when I tell you in a jiffy the women turned up the skirts of their best dresses, got out their big aprons, and went to work to get their dinner. They had everything with them — chickens, rabbits, vegetables, tinned things, bread, and even charcoal. A kind welcome had made them cheerful, and before nine o'clock they were all established at an improvised table on the roadside, eating, chatting and *laughing*. It was a sight that did us all good.

It was not much after ten when the women went to bed, leaving the men to clear up and re-pack. It was a family of neighbours — rich shop keepers, hotel keepers, and their farm hands, and farmers. One man told me that he alone had left fifty thousand francs' worth of materials behind him, and his only prayer was that the Allies had been able to take it or destroy it. There was no sign of class distinction. They were all one family, and had all such pretty manners. The baby — about three — came to offer her little hand when she was put to bed, and lisp her "*Bon soir, Madame, et bonne nuit,*" and one after another of the group came into the garden to say good-night.

The elderly man remarked that it would be pleasant to sleep out of the sound of the guns. I had to laugh, as I replied:

"Well, I am sorry that we cannot promise you that. We are just in front of the guns of the outer forts of Paris, and we get a Gotha visit almost every night."

But that idea did not disturb them. They had been accustomed to so much worse. And sure enough, we had hardly got into bed, when, at about twenty minutes past eleven, the guns began to fire from the forts, and for an hour and a quarter the noise was infernal.

I was up early this morning, but, as I wanted to keep the house quiet, in order that my tired guests might sleep, I came upstairs to write to you. The news is bad — the Germans are in Soissons again, and the Allied army is still retreating south and west. Poor Soissons! This makes the third time its people have had to get out. I remember so well that day in the end of August — the twenty-ninth, I think — in 1914, when the British lost it the first time. But a fortnight later people were returning, though they did not stay long, as the following January the Germans began bombarding it, and it was not until March, 1917, that the town was again safe for civilians, and now, for the third time, these poor people are wanderers again.

Well, my guests are beginning to move about. Amélie is calling me to my coffee, and I will finish this later.

Later

All sorts of things have happened since I went down to breakfast. I have only time to add a few words to this. News has come that the railroad is cut — for civilians — at Meaux. There is no certainty that even that communication with Paris will not at any moment become impossible. I am leaving for Paris — only for twenty-four hours — at five o'clock.

I will write to explain from there. In the meantime there is no need for you to worry *yet.* In case of any change in my plans I shall cable so that you will know where I am. I shall time the cable to reach you before this letter does so that you will not be left in any uncertainty. In case you have received no word by wire when this reaches you, you are to understand that I am back here, and all is well.

XXIV

5 Villa Victor Hugo, Paris, June 1, 1918

WELL, here we are, in practically the same situation as on that memorable September day in 1914, when Amélie and I made our rush to Paris, to return the same night and find the British army at the gate, at the end of that tragic two weeks' retreat from Mons.

This is what happened.

The cordial welcome that my neighbours gave the refugees who arrived Thursday on the hilltop braced them up and consoled them at the end of their two days' pilgrimage in the heat and dust, and their calm and courage braced us all up. But alas! the bad news of Friday morning spoiled all that. When I went into the garden after my coffee, I found them in the road at the gate, with their heads over a newspaper examining a map of the front. I was not especially surprised when the leader came into the garden a little later, and said:

"Well, Madame, although you were all so kind as to urge us last night to rest here to-day and not go on until to-morrow, we have decided that it is hardly wise. We are leaving at once, and making for Melun. The roads are crowded now, and it seems to us most unsafe here. We hope to reach Melun during the night."

Two hours later they were gone.

Not long after, while I was sitting in the garden, listening to the confused noises from the moving trains of refugees on the road, and trying to make up my mind calmly what it was wisest to do, Amélie came out, and began to argue the matter with me. To my surprise I found that her mind was fixed on having me go to Paris at least, and wait there for the turn of the tide — for turn it must. I don't really know why it must, but I feel that it will. All her arguments did not seem sound, but some of them were wise enough.

She argued that every one had gone but the farmers and peasants; that the situation was different from that of 1914; that then I belonged to the most powerful of the neutral countries, whereas to-day I belonged to the most hated of Germany's enemies; that even if we were not invaded we risked being bombarded; that in case of a bombardment they could all live in the subterranean passages, and not mind it too much, but that it would be unnecessarily uncomfortable for me; that I could still get to Paris with a trunk, but in case of a hurried evacuation later I would have to go without clothes — and finally, as a crowning argument, she said,

"We all want you to go, and we shall feel less anxious when you are in a safer place."

I heard her out, but I was doing some pretty tall thinking. One thing was certain — I had to have money. Was n't history repeating itself? It was already taking three and sometimes four days to get a letter into Paris, and almost as many to get one out. That meant that it would take nearly a week to get money by mail, and communications might be cut at any minute. Besides, Amélie was quite right on one point, — it might be prudent for me to have a trunk in Paris, so that, in case we were ordered out, I could at least find clean clothes at the end of my voyage.

Finally I cut the argument short.

"All right, Amélie," I said. "I 'll go up to Paris. But I shall come right back as soon as I get some money, see how things really are in Paris, and leave my trunk."

"Good," said Amélie, jumping up. "Pack the trunk at once. There is a train at five. I 'll harness in an hour. That will give you time enough, and we must allow for the crowd on the road."

I protested that the next morning would do, but she insisted that it was possible that the next morning I might not be able to get away. I did n't believe it, but, in the end, I took the five o'clock train — that was day before yesterday, the day on which I last wrote to you.

We started away silently, except that I assured every one who came out to say good bye to me that there was no good bye, as I was coming back, surely no later than Monday. But as we drove across the Chemin Madame I was surprised to find that Amélie was crying, a thing she rarely does. When I leaned forward to smile into her face she quite broke down.

"You must not try to come back. None of us want you to. It is too dangerous. After this is all over we can find one another again. We will do all that we can to save your house and all your things."

"Nonsense," I replied, "of course I am coming back! You are to go to Couilly to fetch me at two o'clock on Sunday, and, in case I am not there, at the same hour Monday, when I shall surely be there. In the meantime, if I can telegraph, I will. Do you understand?"

"I understand that you are coming *if you can get back*."

"Fudge," I replied, but I knew that I was taking that chance, so I hurriedly gave her certain instructions in case our hill was evacuated; emptied what money I had on me into her lap; carefully wrote out a couple of addresses, in and out of Paris, where she could reach me; arranged what was to be done about all the beasties in case worse came to worst, and the one consolation I felt was that in case Amélie was right and I wrong about the situation I could certainly serve them better by going than staying. If a bombardment drove them down into the caves I should be an embarrassment to them. If military orders drove them into the roads, why there were a horse and donkey and two covered wagons, and again they would be more at ease without me, while outside the zone I could help them better than inside, and prepare a refuge for them.

But as I stood on the steps at the station watching Amélie drive away I knew that she was still crying—her mind made up for the worst. I simply refused to consider that it could happen. I was not gay. Who could be? You never saw such a sight as the *gare* was. The refugees who had arrived thus far on foot, with their pitiful bags and parcels, were being taken on by the railroad. Hundreds of women and children from Couilly and St. Germain and Quincy were flying, taking beds and all sorts of boxes and bundles with them. It was 1914 all over again, only a hundred times sadder.

At Esbly, where we changed cars, it was even worse.

The train from Meaux was over an hour and a half late. The platform was piled with boxes and bundles, trunks and baby-carriages loaded with parcels, baskets and rolled-up bedding. The crowd was as sad-looking as the baggage — women leading children and dogs, carrying bundles of all sorts, and string-bags in which shoes and bread were conspicuous. There were birds in cages, and cats crying in baskets. The sight did not tend to make anyone gay.

It was a strangely silent crowd that stood during that hour and a half of weary waiting while train after train of rolling stock from up the line was hurried towards Paris, and train after train of military material was rushed through to Meaux. When the train, which should have come at twenty minutes to six, finally pulled in at almost half-past seven it seemed to me that I was back at that day in 1914, — over forty-five months ago.

If the trip to town had not had some encouraging moments I am afraid that I might have arrived in Paris in a mood not far removed from that in which I had left Amélie at Huiry.

The crowd in the packed compartment, in which I found a place, was interesting. There was a family from Nancy, which had been stopping at Meaux, there was an *infirmière* from the big military hospital, Val de Grace, and people flying from Meaux, and the principal topic of conversation was, quite naturally, the "boys from the States."

The greatest anxiety of every one but the nurse was that the delay of the train would force them to remain over night in bombarded Paris.

We should have been in Paris before seven o'clock. We got there at ten minutes to nine.

All along the line we had been side-tracked or held up to let long military trains have the right of way—trains packed with *poilus*—those closed cars marked "*hommes,* 40, *chevaux,* 8;" you remember them?—with men sitting in the open doors, their feet hanging out, all smoking and laughing, trains *camouflé* with splashes of green and dirt-coloured paint; trucks on which were mounted all sorts of cannon, their noses in the air, trains of ammunition wagons, trains of trucks carrying huge gas-tanks with all sorts of cautionary directions in huge letters, and, finally, as we drew out of Vaires and stopped, we came alongside of the first train *blindé* and the first tanks I had ever seen. The huge armoured train—*camouflé,* of course—consisted of four enormous cars, and each had its lower car for the gunners. On the lower roofs sat the men, singing and laughing—most of them in their shirt-sleeves—extraordinary for French boys—and each car had its mascot. On one was a white lamb, with a ribbon about his neck. On one was a monkey. On one was a white poodle, who looked as if he had just had a bath. On the fourth was a bird in a cage.

Somehow all this bucked me up tremendously. Every one was hanging out of the car windows. There was a hearty exchange of courtesies. There was no sign of anything but high faith and cheery good humour on the faces of any of these men, who, inside a very few hours, would probably be in the thick of it. I drew a long breath as I thought to myself, "Well, the French are not all dead *yet*. With spirit like this they ought to be able to stem the tide."

The scene at the station in Paris beggared all description. Never since the war began have I seen anything like it. The baggage was piled, pell-mell, on the platforms. It had been apparently many days since there had been any empty space in the baggage rooms. One had to pick one's way through it to find an exit. I found an old porter who knew me to carry my bag, and gave him a receipt for my trunk. He shook his head and advised me not to try to get it that night, as it would surely be hours before I could find it, and by that time it would be impossible to get a cab, as it would be dark, and cabs do not care to make long trips after dark, when a Gotha attack is an almost nightly occurrence. There seemed to be nothing else to do, although, as I looked about, I saw no reason why anyone could not help himself to a good-looking small trunk like mine and walk off with it.

When we got outside there was no cab in sight, and a crowd waiting. So the old man told me to stay right where I was — not budge, no matter what happened, even if he should be ten minutes. So there I stood fixed in the twilight, watching the scene. Now and then a *taxi-auto* would come in through the gate. Instantly twenty people would rush to meet it. It was a real case of short distance sprinting and no favour.

But that did not interest me as much as the big *camions* of the American Red Cross which have done most of the rescue work during this evacuation. The refugees who arrive at this station, after they have been fed and cleaned, are carried by these big *camions* to the stations on the lines going out to the south and west. It was exciting for Parisians to see these great open *camions,* with sturdy American lads in their sombreros, in their shirt-sleeves, — with the sleeves rolled to the elbows at that, — standing braced on widespread feet, with their arms folded, as the autos bumped over the pavements.

It was not ten, but twenty, minutes before my old porter finally came back, riding on the running-board of a taxi. I was glad to see him, I can tell you. It was already dark. It was ten o'clock when I reached my destination, and I had left home at four, and had had no dinner—not that this is very important in these days.

I had not even got through talking when the *alerte* sounded. But this is getting to be a common occurrence, so that it would not be worth recording, if it had not been a rather unusual raid. It was quarter to eleven when the first gun fired, and fifty-five minutes later came the *berloque*. But while the "all clear" was being bugled in the streets there came a second *alerte,* and for a few minutes the *sirène* and the B-flat bugle did a duet, and I assure you it was comic. People who had started from the *abris* said the whole thing was very funny—the bugler lowered his bugle,—the fireman began tooting his horn,—people who had come out of the cellars ran back—anyway, here are more points for the future makers of farce-comedy.

After it was all over we stood for a while on the balcony listening to the church bells ringing out the message "all clear" in the suburbs. It sounded so pretty. It is a pity that so alluring a sound in the night should be associated with anything so sinister. On our hill, the *alerte* is given by *tolling* the bells. I don't enjoy that. We have no "all clear" signal. We know when the forts stop firing that it is over.

As soon as I had my trunk in Paris I

wanted to go right home again. I found real comfort in the fact that if I were driven out of my home I should have at least a change of shoes — they are so costly just now — seventy-five francs a pair for shoes that in the old days cost twenty-five. But since I was in town it seemed wise to look the situation over carefully and provide for possibilities. One thing was certain — if I were actually forced out by military operations, with which neither fear nor my own wishes had anything to do, why then Paris would be no place to stay.

There is not in my mind the smallest chance of Paris ever being taken or besieged. But there is a chance that, if the Germans pass Compiègne, they can mount the guns which bombarded Antwerp, and still pound Dunkirk, and Paris may, for a few days, be seriously bombarded. In case of that possibility becoming a fact, I imagine that few of us foreigners would be allowed to stay in Paris, and I have spent all day to-day, which is Sunday, arranging for that eventuality, — that is to say, all except what has been spent writing you this long letter.

XXV

June 4, 1918

WELL, here I am at home again, and I have been very busy ever since I got here, most of the time chuckling. Life is not all tragic, and it is only a breath over the line to laughter, as usual.

I came back on Monday, the second, as I said I should. The drive on Paris at both Château-Thierry and Compiègne seems to be held up. The Boches are in Château-Thierry, and they have crossed the Marne at Dormans, southeast of Château-Thierry, but they are still outside Compiègne. Yesterday was the eighth day of the big battle, and it almost appears to be a rule that an eight days' drive is about all an army can stand.

The trip back was what it always is in these days, as almost the only soldiers I meet on the train are the boys from the States. But they are not much given, just now, to talk. They know little about the country, and their one desire seems to be to get on to the job, get it done, and get home. Besides, in spite of anything one can do, there is a different feeling in one's heart towards them. The French and English seem hardened to it, and take it all as a matter of course. The boys from the States do not, *yet*.

I found Amélie waiting at the station. She was visibly surprised to see me. It was quite evident that she had not expected me. She drove me up the hill quite sadly, and her only comment was:

"Now you 'll have to do it all over again. I was comfortable, knowing you were safe, and now I 've got to go through it all again."

When I got to the house, the moment I opened the door I discovered one reason for her discomfort at my return. The house was dismantled. My first impulse was to scold, but when I realized how hard they must all have worked, and with what good intention, I decided to laugh loud and long instead.

I wish you could have seen the house. There was not a curtain. There was not a dish in the dining-room nor in the kitchen. The mirrors were down, and pictures on the floor, faces to the wall. My winter clothes, all the bed and body linen and even kitchen towels had been packed, and everything carried up the hill and hidden underground. My first impulse as I looked about the dismantled home was to be very cross, but, before I opened my mouth I looked into the library. There stood my books all along the walls. She had not dared touch them. The hearty laugh the sight simply knocked out of me gave me time to appreciate it. As soon as I could get my face straight I said: "Oh, Amélie, Amélie! And you said, in 1914, that nothing would ever induce you to do a thing like this again!"

"Well, mistress," she replied, "it's *your* things I've hidden this time," which was perfectly true. Her own home had not been touched.

There was no reply to be made to that except that I was grateful to her for leaving me something to read and my typewriter. She had hidden the phonograph.

She explained that she saw no way to hide the books, as there were not cases enough or time enough — and she reasoned that if the house were destroyed, and evidently she had made up her mind to that, I *could* go on without books, but that I would be glad to have bedding and dishes and clothes. I saw her point of view. She did not see mine.

So you can guess how I am living. Amélie has made me up one bed with her sheets. I drink my coffee out of a bowl, and stir it with a pewter spoon. I have two plates and a knife and fork from her house. I know a little of discomforts of which, up to now, I have had none. I am going to support it a few days. I really have not the heart to order all that hard work done over again at once, especially as Amélie is not yet sure that I may not have to leave.

The atmosphere is anything but calm here. Meaux was bombarded yesterday, and more harm done in an hour than during the entire battle of the Marne. In addition, one of the first *régiments du choc*, the boys who fell back in the first hours of the attack of May 27 — less than two hundred are left of the regiment — came here to rest before retiring further to reorganize. Naturally they arrived in a sadly demoralized condition, in a *commune* rather demoralized already. It was an unfortunate combination. It was the first time that the *poilus* had ever brought anything but courage, hope and gaiety into the place.

Yet let me tell you a strange thing. Even with Amélie, whose mind is made up that we are to be invaded, that idea does not for a moment mean that she believes in a defeat. It does not do even to say to her "the Germans are so strong." Any speech like that arouses her anger. She replies with a vicious emphasis:

"They are no stronger than we are. If they are, why have they not beaten us, when they were ready, and we were not, when they are so much more numerous than we are, and have three times as many guns?" And they have, you know. But that does not prevent one from dreading an invasion all the same.

As long ago as the first weeks of the war I wrote you that I could not foresee a defeat for France, and that I believed that even if her armies were beaten back to Bordeaux, with their backs against the Biscay, I was convinced they would still hold out. Of course they could not have, if all the world had not come to their aid, but is n't it a legitimate matter of pride that France, as a nation and as a people, has made herself so dear to the affections of the world, and the cause for which she stands so just, that twenty governments have ranged themselves beside her, so that even though Paris be taken, even though the army of France be wiped out, Germany would have no chance to win, for all the United States will come over before that can happen.

I sometimes wonder if it is possible for you to understand just what it means to be French to-day? The men from the States, great as their sacrifice is, leave their women and children in security. The men of France, standing out there in that battle-line, have not that comfort, for, while they are offering their lives for the cause, right over their heads the enemy is sending death to their very firesides. Startling idea, is n't it?

Our roads are full of moving artillery— Americans passing everywhere, and the enthusiasm for them grows every day.

The heavy artillery was very noisy at noon. But we are so used to that that we are nervous without it. When we don't hear it every one here thinks nothing is doing, and that, in spite of the fact that we all know the present battle is a battle of movement, an infantry battle, the sort of battle in which the French are most at home.

It looks to-night as if Compiègne were safe, although it has suffered badly from the artillery fire. Do you remember the last day we were there, and lunched at the handsome new hotel at the entrance of the forest, with its wide verandah and its awnings — so much more English than French, — and how we drove through the forest to take tea at Pierrefonds? I remember it was a hunts day, and every little way, down the long vistas of trees, we saw the huntsmen dashing across, and heard the horns. It is a lovely memory. Though the town is so badly hurt, we are told the palace, with its souvenirs of Napoleon III, has been spared by order of the Kaiser, as it was there he planned to make his last rest on the route to Paris, to put on his white uniform *de parade,* and take his automobile for the fortifications, where his war-horse was to wait him and carry him into Paris, and through the Arc de Triomphe, — another of those illusions already twice destroyed, since he waited outside Nancy, ready to enter. It has been a close shave each time, but "a miss is as good as a mile."

XXVI

June 22, 1918

THINGS have not changed much since I wrote you. The battle seems for the moment stationary, but we all know that it is only held up until the Germans can re-organize another *coup*. As that of March 21st extended from Cherizy to the forest of Coucy, and that of May 27th along the tragic Chemin des Dames, from the defences of Soissons to Reims and across the Marne the other side of Château-Thierry, about thirty miles from us, we are unusually nervous right here as to the direction of the next attack. If it should be in the direction of Meaux it would be all up with us.

By a strange chance it is on the sector which includes Château-Thierry that the boys from the States are holding the line and holding it bravely — brilliantly. Isn't it odd to think that while they are all along the line it should be at the point where an advance would menace my house that the "boys from home" should be doing their most conspicuous work? The people about me are really sentimental on the subject. You would think, from their attitude, that I had especially ordered the arrangement. Perhaps I will be mobbed if they don't hold on!

We hear the guns intermittently. There is an almost daily movement of American troops over the *route* to Meaux. I do not see them. We have been dealt three air raids since I last wrote, and now, as we have a *tir de barrage* from five points in an arc about us, the noise of the guns of defence is terrible.

Almost every day a new group of refugees arrive. We have a large number from Acy, near Soissons, and within a mile or two of Sarches, where the Englishwomen who used to be at Meaux, and of whom I think I wrote you, went last fall to organize a big *foyer*. Somehow, in all the excitement of the last month, it was not until the people from Acy arrived that I realized that, of course, the big *foyer* at Sarches must have been destroyed.

It was.

A week ago last Tuesday they surprised me by walking into the garden. They had come over from Meaux, where they stopped in the retreat, to help in the hospital, where they were short of nurses. I am afraid they were surprised when they found me here. They insisted that I was not to stay, that the Americans at Meaux sent word that, if I were still here, I was to be told that I was "crazy to stay."

They had passed through a terrible experience, seeing all they had organized so well, and all they had collected and arranged — libraries, music rooms, tennis courts, dear little houses and gardens — destroyed, and had made a tragic retreat over roads full of empty gun-carriages, flying women and children, retreating soldiers, exploding ammunition as the retiring army destroyed its stores to prevent the Germans from getting what could not be carried. They arrived, nerve-tired, at Meaux to go right into the crowded hospital, just in time (they were on night service) to stand to their posts when the air raid on the morning of the third of June did such damage only a short distance from the ambulance. It was no wonder that they were a bit pessimistic about our chances here. They were sweetly sympathetic about the house and my library, and wanted me to make an effort to get military automobiles to come and take away my treasures before it was too late.

But for that I had no ambition. Military automobiles have too much work to do which is more important, and I thought it would be time enough, if ever, when we were warned to get out.

"But you will get no warning," they exclaimed; "if you wait for that it will be too late."

But my mind was made up. I have often

wondered what would become of all the stuff I have collected about me when I have done with it. Don't you remember, even in the old days before I came out here, I used to laugh about it with you? A poor person's library, got together haphazard, is like one's collection of friends, — no one else wants it. I 'd hate the idea of its being sold, and turning up for years after in the dusty boxes on the *quais,* as I have, in my time, found the books of others. Well, if it were to go up in smoke, as my sacrifice for the victory, I shan't care. In fact, it will be a fine end, and settle one anxiety in my mind.

They insisted so much about, at least, *my* leaving that I was glad to be able to tell them that I was going to Paris next day, and I did not tell them that I was coming directly back — but I did.

I was glad I went, for I had a most interesting trip, and saw thousands of our boys. I don't see much of them unless I do move about a bit, for they just rush by here to Château-Thierry.

I went up last Friday. On the *route de Meaux,* as I drove down to the station, I found the road simply full of *camion*-loads of the boys from home. As Ninette walked slowly along the line, I leaned out to call my greeting to the boys in English. I wish you could have seen their smiling faces. It took Ninette half an hour to go from the top of the hill down to the station, and I did my best to give them a solo acclamation all the way, and they returned the compliment.

As my train ran into Esbly, we passed carload after carload, side-tracked outside the station, all in their shirt-sleeves, sitting in the cattle-cars which carry the French troops, eating their breakfast in picnic fashion. I longed to run back down the track to greet them, but I had not time, so I bought up all the English papers I could get — a few Paris *Heralds* and *Daily Mails* — and sent them down by the station-master, who was only too glad to make the trip.

The excitement in the station was intense. Every one was crowded on the end of the platform from which the train-load of Americans could be seen. You would have thought, from their air, that the war would be over day after to-morrow. You should have seen their faces and heard the tone of their voices when they spoke of "*ces braves garçons de l'Amérique.*" I told you at the time that war was declared in Washington that we were a lucky people. Our boys have come over to cast the deciding vote in a long-tied struggle. They are going to get credit for that decision. Please God they'll play up to the enthusiasm there is for them, — and modestly do full justice to the great sacrifices which have prepared the road for them.

It is lucky that in these days I rarely read in the train — the road is too interesting — otherwise I should have missed seeing the groups of lads from the States bivouacked all along the line, lying on the banks or grouped about eating. I rode most of the way at the open window, waving my greetings, and they not only always waved back as cordially as if they had known I was a fellow citizen, but often rose to their feet to do it.

I found Paris quiet, — it was the fifteenth, and the big gun had ceased firing on the twelfth, and there had been no air raids for nine nights. But on Sunday night there was a terrible one, in which there were lives lost and a big fire started. It began at twenty minutes after eleven and lasted until one o'clock — long enough to spoil the night.

On the train Monday I read the news that the big offensive for Venice had begun, so there is one more cause for hourly suspense, but the worst seemed to be over in three days — this time the Italians are holding.

The weather has been queer. For a month here we had practically no rain, and everything is drying up. My lawn is a pitiful sight, but that is no matter. What does matter are the potatoes and beans.

Last night we had a most remarkable sunset. I never saw anything at all like it, or anything of the sort that was so strangely beautiful. The western horizon was like the flames of a huge fire — copper and gold with a background of sullen red. From the point where the sun was sinking started broad clouds like banners, extending in even rays, like the spokes of a wheel, up to the zenith and paling down to the east. These cloud rays were almost white on one edge and blackish gray on the other. They were even in width, and as evenly spaced as if done with a compass, and they curved with the dome of the heavens. Every one was out on the hill to watch the spectacle, and if I had seen it in a picture and not with my own eyes, I could not have believed it to be a true bill.

XXVII

June 29, 1918

I GOT up this morning feeling as if I had never had a trouble in the world. All my nervousness had disappeared in the night. I 'd like to think that it presages something remarkable. I am afraid it only means that I slept from ten to six without budging, — which is unusual. You can guess how sound my sleep was when I tell you that there was a raid last night, and I never heard it. I am generally a light sleeper. I never expected to arrive at sleeping through a bombardment. But I have. So it may be that I am getting used to it. I am willing, for it 's small service I can render listening to the racket. I can't stop the bombs, nor bring down the Gothas, though if wishing it on them would accomplish it they would long ago have been all annihilated.

It has been rather a busy and picturesque week.

Last Sunday — that was the twenty-third — we had the 304th dragoons camped here for the night — the very biggest *cantonnement* we have ever had, and I had the Captain in the house.

They arrived at six o'clock, and it was one of the hottest days I ever saw. They had been in the saddle since four in the morning.

The quartermaster and a couple of corporals had been here all day preparing the *cantonnement*. We had eighty horses in the little railed-in pasture on the top of the hill, which we never thought was too big for Ninette and Bijou, and fifty in the smaller one where we used to put the goat. These two little *parcs,* as *Père* calls them, are on either side of the *devise,* a bit of City of Paris land following the line of the Paris water conduits from the Ourcq to Paris, and across it runs a footpath, always kept clear, which is barred at regular distances so that it resembles a hurdle-course, though it is only for pedestrians.

I never had such respect or understanding for the tremendous work required to keep an army going as I had while I watched that regiment arrange itself just for this *étape* of ten hours. Every one knew just what to do. In less than an hour after the head of the line came into the courtyard at *Père's* where the kitchens and big commissary wagons were set up, all was in order.

I sat on a big stone beside the road and, while the horses were being led in a line to the watering-troughs, I saw the speed with which posts four feet high attached with heavy cords were driven into the ground some ten feet apart along both sides of the footpath. To these posts such of the horses as could not be stabled or put into our little enclosures, were attached by their halters. It took almost less time than it takes me to write it for saddles to be removed, nose bags to be adjusted, and there, close around the four sides of the enclosures, and almost shoulder to shoulder down either side of the footpath, the horses ate, while saddles were being inspected and piled in regular heaps in the centre of the enclosure and against the barriers on the outside. Every one was busy, there was plenty of *blague* falling about, but no one seemed to get into anyone's way, and by nine o'clock everybody was eating.

My! but it takes lots to feed them. They threw whole beeves out of the big *camion,* — an old Paris tram-car, if you please, with windows replaced by wire screenings, inside which the beef and mutton hung up just as it does at the butcher's, — while whole kegs of beer had a *camion* of their own, and the vegetable kettles were almost as big as barrels.

While the dinner was preparing, and a huge dish of eggs which it took two men to carry was being cooked in my kitchen, the men washed up wherever they could find a place. I suppose you have heard that the *poilu* never washes unless he has to. It is a standard joke. There are exceptions. You ought to have seen the court at Amélie's, and what I sarcastically call my *basse cour.*

Long ago, when I thought I'd raise geese —I never told you about that, perhaps?— one of my follies—for lack of a brook I bought a huge, flat, round bathtub. It was a metre and a half in diameter. When I gave up raising geese the tub was put in the tool house, and there it stood on end. The *poilus* found it. Just as I was coming through the long garden at Amélie's, which runs beside the chickens' home, with only a high *grillage* between, a loud voice warned me with: "*Attention. Défense d'entrer. Salle de bain privée,*" and I got through the gate in time to avoid a study in the nude. Amélie explained when I got through that they were sprinkling one another in the tub with the big watering-pot.

They were still eating when I went to bed.

As I closed up for the night I thought to myself "It is dollars to doughnuts that the Gothas will come to-night." And just before eleven they did, and the *barrage* was not silent until midnight.

Amélie told me in the morning that the boys simply put out their lights, and finished cleaning and repacking in the dark.

Just imagine how much actual work all this means, when I tell you that at three o'clock the next morning they were up and at work, and at half-past three they were in the saddle, and the long line of cavalry and the big commissary wagons and the ammunition train, with its mule-drawn *mitrailleuses,* were trotting and rattling on the road again.

We had one day's rest and then the 102nd artillery came in for the same sort of a repose. It was a different kind of *cantonnement,* of course, as there were no horses except those of the officers; everything else — men, cannon, ammunition, equipment — was carried on *camions* and in lorries. But the little road in front of my house has never been so picturesque. All along that road from the turn above the well at Amélie's to that below where it goes into Voisins, in front of Mademoiselle Henriette's, a line of *camions* carrying guns was drawn up, and in the open space in front of my gate the ammunition wagons were simply packed. In this *étape* there were no kitchens and no commissary. The men each carried one day's rations, and the officers rode down to the hotel at Couilly to dine.

I thought, as I looked out of my bedroom window, that night, "*Là! là!* if the Gothas get this to-night they will make a mess." But they did not. And before daylight the next day they were off.

We are still waiting for some sign of the next movement at the front, and of course all this military activity means something.

The artillery had hardly got away when

news came that the 21st dragoons were coming in, and while I was talking to the Captain's orderly, who was arranging the officers' quarters here, and I was explaining the kitchen to the cook — for four officers were to eat in the house — I got a telegram from Paris telling me to come up without delay, as I was wanted at the Embassy. So I had just time to welcome the Captain as he rode in, and catch the noon train.

I went directly to the Embassy, where I was informed that, at the request of the French Government, all strangers were being asked to leave Paris as well as the war zone. The explanation given was that while no one thought it possible that the Germans could get to Paris, it was possible — perhaps probable — that Paris would be bombarded. As far as I was personally concerned they considered my situation untenable, as even a slight advance on the Marne would bring me within fifteen miles of the firing line, where I would be an embarrassment to the army, — in fact, though they put it more politely, a nuisance. All my papers had to be examined and *viséd,* and I had to select a place to go, which was properly written against my name in the list of Americans allowed, in the last combing out, to remain in France, and then I was told that, as I lived in the *zone des armées,* and travelled at the pleasure of the Fifth army corps, I would have to go to the French bureau which controlled circulation on the railroads, and get a French *visé*.

Before we left the house we had agreed that if it became necessary to leave the town we would go to Versailles, as a first *étape*. It is outside the fortifications to the southwest, and in case of need it would be easier to retreat west from there than from the city proper. Of course what the authorities are really trying to do is to avoid the possibility of a panic at the railway stations at the last minute in case the town is bombarded. There are plenty of people who will not take this warning seriously, but a great number will, and the fewer people there are in the city the better.

The passport department had been crowded. It was evident that they were combing people out carefully. I had only escaped hours of waiting on the stairs by being discovered by an old Boston friend who needed a witness to swear to her identity. But, even with that advantage, which admitted me long before my turn, the process was a long one, and my papers were examined by at least six men before I escaped and pushed my way downstairs through the waiting crowd. I had been telegraphed for by a friend as we were called alphabetically.

From the Embassy I went to the French bureau on the rue de Rivoli. There I found the waiting line extending down the street and round the corner, and at that hour of the day the sun shines right into the colonnade. There I stood in the heat, in a pushing line, for an hour before my turn came to even enter the building. When I finally got in and found my proper man, I was told that my papers were in perfect order, that I could go to Versailles whenever I desired. *And* I was told that the sooner I left Paris the better. I took the advice forty-eight hours later, but I did not go to Versailles, I came back here. I tell you all this just to show you what it is like to be here now. There is an even chance either way, that's all.

I stayed in town Wednesday and Thursday night, and came home yesterday. On both nights there was a bad air raid. That on Wednesday destroyed a big shop which we both know, and that on Thursday was the noisiest I have heard since March, and one of the most destructive. It began at half-past nine and lasted until midnight, and the bombs seemed to be distributed over a wide area. Just as in the big March raid I had happened, by accident, on one of the bombarded regions, so yesterday morning I went through another on my way to the station — the Place Vendôme. But all the damage I could see was a terrible destruction of window glass. There was hardly a whole pane in the square.

On arriving at Couilly I found the road up the hill full of ammunition *camions*, and Ninette climbed up with the huge *camions* full of big *obus* crawling by. I own to have felt foolishly nervous as they jerked slowly along. I felt as if, should one backslide or topple over, I should see Kingdom-come before this cruel war was over. Of course I knew they would n't, but we have had some queer accidents on that road since the great activity which has never ceased began on May twenty-sixth.

I found the 21st dragoons had gone. Amélie said they had seemed very happy — the officers — and I imagine they had a better time than if I had been at home, for they had the freedom of the house and no fear that they were putting its mistress out. Amélie said they did not leave the garden at all — that they read and played cards and wrote and chatted all day, and had their coffee out on the lawn; but I found a little note, tucked into the drawer in the salon table, from the Captain, saying:

"Please read here the cordial thanks and respectful homages of a Captain who was bitterly disappointed that his charming hostess, as soon as he had set eyes on her, disappeared."

Really, are n't they wonderful? It is not only that they feel the necessity to do that sort of thing, but that they are so unconscious and do it so well, and sign it all up with their names and rank.

I told you that I was feeling very chipper when I began this, and I am. I wish I knew why. It is not only that; I simply ordered Amélie this morning to set my house in order. I don't care how many people she gets to help her. It must be done at once. She argues that since things are put away they may as well stay until we are sure of the next move, but I say "No," and when I say it loud like that I am always obeyed.

Besides, just to show you how well I feel, I have decided to go to Paris both for the Fourth and the Fourteenth of July. Paris is going to make our Independence Day a national fête, and on the Fourteenth I shall know that somewhere you will be watching the States celebrating Bastille Day at the same time that I am standing somewhere in Paris cheering the Allies. Well, of course, not exactly that, because really I shall be in the streets while you are still sleeping at two in the morning, and I shall be at tea when you see your procession start, but that's not important. The Allied spirit of the thing is what matters. This is a great decision for me. You know how I hate a crowd. But there will be few more things of this sort left for me, and I do feel that perhaps this is the first scene in the last act. You see how very much on the right side of the bed I got out this morning.

XXVIII

July 12, 1918

WELL, I can tell you this is dry season. If it were important I should grieve over my garden. You should see my dahlias. I don't ask them to be superb until later, but they never came up in such a state as they have this year. The slugs ate them as fast as they came out of the ground, in spite of the fact that, armed with the tongs, I picked them up carefully twice a day. Such dirty slimy things, all sizes and all colours, from little pale white things and ditto black up to big fat yellow fellows and ditto brown, with horrid heads like seals and bulging eyes, which they draw in and close when you touch them. In spite of all that hard and disagreeable work the first leaves were all eaten and the first buds to open are small, because of the lack of water, and worse than that, they are half eaten away by the slugs. But never mind, I had the fun of playing at gardening, and now I can busy myself doctoring them. We have had every variety of weather this week. It was piping hot on Sunday, it blew hard on Tuesday, was clear and sunny like an autumn day on Wednesday, it showered on Thursday, it opened and shut on Friday, it pours to-day. Variety, anyway. In spite of the terrible drought of which the farmers complain with reason, and which has dwarfed all my posies and scorched my lawn yellow, the grain looks well, and I have never heard the larks sing as they sing these mornings and evenings, as I watch them mounting and mounting, their rippling notes falling out of the clouds long after the bird is invisible. And there are so many finches. There is one who sits and gives a real concert on the ridge-pole of the house every day, and I am just as nice an audience as I know for him — always with an eye that Khaki does not sneak up there, for I suspect Khaki and doubt if he makes any distinction between birds that sing and birds that don't, when he goes a-hunting.

You ask me if the winter is going to be a hard one. Well, to tell you the truth, except that I know it is to be another winter with the army "out there," I have not thought much about it. Anyway, what were hardships for four winters will not be so bad this winter, because I am used to them, and expect nothing else. I am getting in wood every day. It is easier to get it than it has been in the previous war years, and I am buying it everywhere, and shall as long as I can find any place to put it. What the army is going to say I don't know, for there is a board on my gate which announces billets for one officer and twenty men, and I am afraid my wood is filling up the soldiers' bedrooms. But I suppose we'll find some way out of it. Perhaps the army will settle it by taking my wood away.

We have heard the artillery at the front almost every day since I last wrote to you, but the newspapers say nothing which explains. The soldiers, going through, say "Don't worry. All is going well. In eight days you can expect to get good news," and that has to content us for the present.

On Monday of last week we had an air raid, which began at quarter before eleven and lasted until nearly two the next morning —that was the first day of this month— and the next morning, at half-past seven, while I was in the garden, there was a heavy *tir de barrage,* but it appeared to be directed to the protection of Meaux, though it was impossible to be sure, in spite of my hearing the Boche machine distinctly. As spent shot began to rattle on the roof, I thought it prudent to take to cover.

The next day I went up to Paris to pass the Fourth, as I wrote you I should. Before I left I made sure that our two *communes* and Huiry itself had American flags, and left Amélie to fling the Stars and Stripes to the French breezes over the gate here and under the bedroom windows, and on the road side of her house. That is all the fête there will be here, but it is enough.

The Fourth was a lovely day. Every one had anticipated, and even the papers had not hesitated to say, that it was more than likely that the Boches would consider the national fête-day of the States, to be gloriously celebrated in the streets of the French capital, as a legitimate opportunity to bring into play again their long-distance cannon. But the Kaiser, if he expected that possibility would keep anyone from going into the streets to see the boys from the States march down the Champs-Elysées, had another disappointment.

We had no desire to hear the discourses nor to see the statesmen sitting in the official tribunes—the former we could read later, and the latter were an old story. We had instead a desire to see the crowd in the street and the movement and watch the reception of the troops at various points of the short march from Washington's monument at the head of the newly christened Avenue President Wilson to the Strasbourg monument on the Place de la Concorde.

The streets in the vicinity of the line of march were crowded, and everywhere, even in the quiet and deserted streets of the other quarters, were the American flags. There was no shop too small to show one. *Bonnes* on the way to market had the Stars and

Stripes on their market baskets. Every taxicab was decorated with the flag, and so was every decrepit old *sapin*. It floated on the tram-cars and the omnibuses, it hung out of almost every window, and at the entrance of the big apartment houses, already closed but for the presence of the *concierge*. Crippled soldiers distributed tiny flags on all the streets. We took ours, two steps from the door, from a one-legged *chasseur Alpin,* who ran about on his peg as lively as a cricket, and as gay — only twenty-two he told me, three years' service stripes on his sleeve, and a *croix de guerre* and *médaille militaire* on his breast, and he laughed in my face when I looked grave as he pinned a flag on me, and remarked, "Don't you mind, I'm not done with them yet;" and away he hopped across the street to pin an American flag on some one else.

We took a cab and drove along the line looking, from our higher elevation, over the heads of the crowds behind each barrier, as no one could approach without a ticket to within a block in any direction of the grandstand — there was only one. My object was to see the cortège passing down the Champs-Elysées from the Rond Point to the Place de la Concorde. So we drove to the Avenue Gabriel, and, close to the garden entrance to the Presidential residence we got out and walked across the garden between the Ambassadeurs and the Alcazar, now given up to the American work for the aid of the French wounded. You remember just the place, for I know we went there to dine together ten years ago. You remember? We sat at a table in the balcony just opposite the stage, and had what you called "the best table d'hôte dinner for the price" you had ever eaten, and watched a good variety show — or at least I did. I remember that you were more interested in the women walking about in the *couloirs*, and the wonderful clothes. Alas! those days are gone.

On arriving near the Avenue some one helped me mount on to a bench, where, over the heads of the throng massed at the curb, I could look up and down the Avenue, with an American aviator, in a Liberty machine, doing stunts over my head just above the tree-tops, and I assure you I had my heart in my mouth most of the time.

The crowd that packed the line of march was almost as picturesque as the procession. As far as the French went it was, of course, largely women, children, and white-haired men, with a sprinkling of *poilus* on leave, convalescent soldiers — the crippled soldiers had a reserved stand near the head of the route — and a great number of English and American men in khaki — the Red Cross and Y. M. C. A. units, the commissary men, who have their headquarters in the Avenue, and a sprinkling of uniforms of all the nations in arms. The shouts and cheers went up in waves as the *cortège* started far away, but in the Avenue itself only began when the head of the line appeared preceded by the band. Then the cries of "*Vivent les Américains*," "*Vivent nos Alliés*," were cut with the "Hip, hip, hurrah!" of the Americans, and it culminated when the division of the Marines, in their battle-stained uniforms, their soiled but trim knapsacks on their backs, and their battered "tin hats" (the boys who cleared the Bois de Belleau), came into sight. I thought then that the kind of crowd which was gathered that day could not make any more noise than they made for the Americans, who, with their guns on their shoulders, marched as steadily as veterans, though their faces were the faces of boys. But I was mistaken, for, with a fine spirit that I loved, they had justly reserved their most ardent acclamations for their own war-worn troops, and the shouts of "*Vivent nos poilus*," "*Vive la France*," were as near hysterical as anything I have seen in France since the war began. I saw women laughing and crying at the same time, and only able to wave their hands in greeting.

After it was all over, we found our taxi again and drove back up the Avenue. It looked so gay, with the crowds laughing and chatting and flowers everywhere. Paris had needed to see its armies and cheer the boys from the front. It did them more visible good than all the heroic talk can ever do. I know it did me.

I had loved seeing so many of our boys, not only in the procession, but the crowd in the street. I love seeing — good soldiers as they are proving themselves — how little they stand on ceremony in private life. The officers nod to one another instead of saluting. A common soldier or a corporal says "Hulloa, old man," to his lieutenant, with whom he probably went to school. Even in public an officer will sometimes stand uncovered as he talks in the street to a girl friend. It is only something so solemn as the passing of the colours that brings the American boy erect, his heels together, his shoulders squared, his hand at just the proper angle of salute, and when it is over, he slaps his hand on his leg in real regimental fashion — and limbers up to the characteristic American slouch again.

I remarked to an American officer one day, as he lifted his hat to greet me, that he was most unmilitary, and his reply was: "Hell! We American soldiers are only *camoufléd* civilians;" and that is terribly true, added to which they have not worn a uniform long enough to be unconscious in playing the rôle of a soldier.

In spite of all the expectations of an attack

of some sort, the big cannon made no sign, and there was no air raid that night.

I came back on the sixth, which was last Saturday. I had hardly got my hat and coat off when a French officer arrived at my gate to arrange for the *cantonnement* here of the American boys coming out from the *secteur* at Château-Thierry — lads who fought at Bois de Belleau. You should have seen the face of the young American sergeant when I addressed him in English, and told him that I was an American. I don't know which of us was the most excited.

The French officer, who spoke no English and depended on me to help him out, told me that there were seven Americans here to arrange the *cantonnement* for fifteen hundred — a Town Major, a quartermaster, and a few corporals and sergeants, and that the rest were expected Monday morning. They were coming by road, marching on foot, and expected to take two days, in fact they were supposed to have already "come out." They are to rest a few days and go up to Paris the morning of the Fourteenth, to be decorated — the Marines won their *fourragère* in the Bois de Belleau — and to march in the procession.

The weather was terribly hot, so when Monday came and went and there was no sign of the American Marines every one was as disappointed as I was, but we all explained it by the intense heat, which would make marching nearly forty miles no joke to tired soldiers just out of a battle. But Tuesday and Wednesday passed, and the advance guard of the battalion who had arrived here with only three days' rations began to worry a little. They were getting a new kind of taste of war. In the meantime they drifted round one after another to see me, play the phonograph and chat. I am afraid they were rather bored. They spoke little French, though they got on well with the French, and they had guard duty to do, and the Town Major kept strict discipline. But here it is Friday night, and I am leaving for Paris to-morrow to see the celebration of the Fourteenth. I do want to see the armies of all the Allies in the Avenue du Bois, otherwise I would not go until the Americans have come and are comfortably settled.

Amélie is not at all content. She is afraid that she cannot properly replace me. She has made me write a note in English which she is to show any American soldier who comes to the door. It is just a line saying that they are welcome and are to consider the house as "a little piece of home," and make themselves comfortable accordingly. She stood over me while I wrote it on a big sheet of paper, imploring me to write it "very large and very distinct," which shows you what Amélie thinks of my handwriting.

She has pinned it on the blotter. She knows how to say "cum een," and I can imagine her taking them by the sleeve, and leading them up to the desk to read the proclamation. She has made me write "Mildred Aldrich, American," as a signature.

By the way, Amélie's English does not march very rapidly. She can still say "I spek Engleesh vairee vell, oh yees." She says they understand her, but she does not get their reply, and is disappointed when I am not by to hear and tell her what they said. She has also learned to say "Got cigarette?" with a strong interrogatory inflection. You see Amélie loves her cigarette, but she does not like Egyptians, the only thing available just now, when the ordinary French cigarette is not sold to civilians. That works very well. The boys understand, and if they have a cigarette they give it to her. But they more often have a pipe and tobacco. I have told Amélie that she must not do this, as the boys have none too much tobacco for themselves, and I thought I had broken her of it. But the other day there was an officer calling and she went out to look at his big car and admire the *chauffeur*—she thought him so *chic*—and I heard her getting off her "Got cigarette?" When he had gone I reproached her, and she looked grieved as she explained that she did not want his cigarettes—besides he did not have any. When

I desired to know why she had taken the trouble to ask if she did not want any she replied: "*Histoire de parler anglais!*"

I thought that was lovely.

I have an idea that the American Marines are not coming at all. There is a tremendous activity everywhere about us. You know, now, since the Germans reached the Marne again, we are not only *zone des armées* but we are *arrière front*, and never since the war began has the military movement about us been so constant. There are hours of the day when we simply cannot drive on our roads at all. All this means something, and, although I am going up to see the first real war celebration of the Fourteenth, I am going with a feeling that if something does not happen while I am gone, something will all the same happen soon.

You realize, of course, that the next move settles our fate here. So long as the Germans hold Soissons Paris is menaced, so long as they hold Château-Thierry the Marne valley is open to them. In either case our situation is critical. If the next move sees the Germans not only held, but pushed back, all danger to us here is, I am convinced, ended forever.

But whichever way it turns is only locally important. Even if Paris is taken, even if it were possible to wipe out the French army, Germany's situation would not be changed and never will be until she has wiped out the States. But every time I think about it the condition of France seems to me the more remarkable — all her men in the war or in war works, all the rescued population of the invaded districts from the frontier to the Somme and the Marne crowded into the south and west, and millions of Allied soldiers from other countries, with thousands of Red Cross workers of all sorts, and hundreds of thousands of German prisoners, and here we are trying to lead a normal life, and coming precious near to doing it. And strangest of all, the majority of the people are more sane and happier than they have ever been. It is a great disaster. Of course it is. But we are all terribly alive, and it is not at such epochs that the world ever bothers itself to write symposiums on "Is Life Worth Living?", or speculates about "*La Lutte pour la Vie*."

Thanks for the newspaper clipping containing the pen portrait of me sitting on the wheelbarrow on the platform of the railway station at Esbly, on the day I went to Paris to carry my trunk, "with tears in my voice if not in my eyes." I am afraid that touch was the pretty young journalist's poetic license — she was pretty, you know. I am sorry the picture struck you as "pitiful and pathetic." I really am. Come now, what would you have had me do, sitting there among that crowd of women leading children by one hand and lugging such of their poor effects as they had saved? You surely could not have expected that I would do a song and dance simply because, up to date, *my home was safe.* I *was* sad. How could I have been anything else? Only a few hours before I had seen a poor flying woman carrying a dead baby in her arms, and among other objects of my journey to Paris was a visit to the American Red Cross to beg some layettes for newborn babies in our commune—*emigrées* of course—and stuff to make underclothes for women and children who had arrived with only what they had on their backs, for in that retreat of over thirty miles, from Noyon to Château-Thierry, between May 27th and June 4th these poor people were taken by surprise and had no time to save more than their skins and what covered them. Will that explain the "tears in my voice" if they were there?

You ask me for news of Mademoiselle Henriette. Is it possible that in all the excitement of the days since the retreat of March 21 I forgot to tell you that she had gone? She is at Salonica. She left here in March—the very first if I remember. Anyway I have looked up her first note—a postcard—from Toulon, dated March 3, in which she says:

"We sail to-morrow. It is Sunday, and

I have just attended mass on deck. It was pretty and very impressive. Standing in the midst of officers, soldiers and sailors, I had once more the illusion that I too was on active service, and felt once more at home. We are sailing without escort, under the protection simply of the Red Cross, although we have on board a neutral — an officer of the Spanish navy."

Odd that I should have forgotten to tell you this at the time. She is now at Zeitenlick, where the service is very hard; but it is interesting and she is at an age to enjoy novel experiences, even when they have to be paid for with mighty hard work.

XXIX

July 22, 1918

THIS has been such a week of mixed emotions that I have not been able to settle down to write.

I got your cable of congratulation on the "great victory" last night. I shall say what I think of that later. It may surprise you to know that I am not in the humour. We are calm and confident here. We are *not* throwing our hats in the air *yet*. The tension has been terrible, and it is a comfort to know that to-night there is not a German on the south bank of the Marne, and we hope they have crossed it for the last time.

I wrote you, if I remember, the night before the Fourteenth, when I was preparing to go up to town to help celebrate the great day. I went and I enjoyed it.

It was drizzly weather, and when, at nine, I prepared to go out and find a place so near the Porte Dauphine that I could see the Allied armies enter the city from the Bois, I found that no one wanted to go with me, on the plea that it would be prettier to see it with my eyes than go out in a crowd plus a drizzle, which of course was flattering but covered a lazy spirit.

Luckily it stopped raining, and the air was fresh, the sky a little overcast, and there was no dust. It was an ideal day for comfort.

I stay in Paris only five minutes' walk from the entrance to the Bois at the end of the Avenue du Bois. I never saw the city look more beautiful. Nothing had been done to conceal or disfigure its beauty. There were no seats put up along the route, and the only tribune was on the east side of the Avenue — near the Porte — just an enclosed space hung in the traditional red, with reserved seats for the President, the diplomatic corps and the city's guests.

On the same side of the Avenue, a little nearer the Porte, was the colour-stand. All along the street on both sides were the chairs that are always there, only more of them, and a simple wooden barrier behind them prevented people from pushing into the space thus reserved. There was no bunting on any of the houses — nothing in the way of decoration, but the flags of all the Allied nations.

Every inch of space was taken. When I arrived at my place, just behind the colour-stand, the presidential party had already arrived, and I passed behind a long line of the most wonderful automobiles I ever saw (and did not much wonder at hearing some one remark, "Well, it seems there is still some *essence* in Paris!").

Just then the head of the procession began to issue from the trees of the Bois, and approach the Porte. The light was just right for it, and the forest of moving bayonets made a wonderful picture, which I shall never forget. Most of the people in the great crowd had evidently, like me, never seen many of the armies, though most of them had, like me, I suppose, seen individual soldiers of all the Allies. I am sure the American papers have given you a full description of the great *cortège* in which the armies of all the Allies-in-arms for the world's liberty marched for the first time in the city the whole world loves, and which even her enemies envy, and doubtless, by the time you get this, the cinemas will have shown it moving on the screen, for I counted almost as many machines at work as there were nations in the show. But what they cannot give you is the colour, which was atmospherically French, and how much that says, you who love France know, nor can it give you the thrills. I simply adored seeing the flag of each nation approach, and the colours on the Allied stand dip to receive each nation's salute, and the soldiers in the crowd as far as I could see rising to attention with their hands at salute as the flags passed.

Along the barrier, behind the seats, soldiers, mostly American, British and Italian, who were not marching, stood erect braced like bareback riders in their perilous position, and they managed to stand rigid as statues to salute the colours — a fine athletic display.

The handsomest men in the line were, to my mind, the Italians. Their greenish grey uniform is a beautiful colour, and their hats, higher in form than those of the other Allies, are terribly smart. But the sturdy Serbs and the Poles with their new flag, and the Czechs, who sang as they marched, were greeted with thundering cheers. As the Americans were the *clou* of the Fourth of July, the British carried off the honours of the Fourteenth. They made a wonderful showing, so trim, marching as if they had never done anything but parade duty, they who have fought like the bulldogs they are. There were English and Irish, Scotch and Welsh, there were Australians, New Zealanders, the armies of Egypt and India and South Africa. It was a fine show, and none of them were more cheered than the tall ruddy men in kilts marching to the crooning of the pipes. It was so hard to realize that this was a demonstration in the midst of a war, at a time when the enemy was nearer the fortifications of the city than they had been in forty-six months, in a city which had known forty days of bombardment by a German cannon, and could not be sure that the forty-first might not come before the procession disbanded.

It was this spirit that I had gone out to see and I had seen it.

This was the sort of experience one cannot hope to get more than once in a fortunate lifetime, the sort of thing that centuries have not seen, and centuries may never see again. It was the very essence of the spirit which is to carry a righteous cause to victory, and which future ages will have good reason to bless.

As a detachment of French cavalry brought up the rear—for the French divisions had been scattered through the line, acting as escort to their comrades-in-arms, which I thought a pretty idea—the crowd broke up quietly, and, while the echoes of the cheers came back to me, receding with the music as the *cortège* continued its route, I walked slowly back to the house, strangely comforted.

We all knew that we were on the eve of another German offensive, and with the consciousness of the great bound forward of two of the previous ones, it was impossible to be quite free from nervousness, or from the feeling that Paris was in danger. But we had seen the men who were to meet the attack, and seen nowhere anything but courage, so why should we worry?

Personally, I can say that nothing has done me so much good as the two look-ins I have taken in Paris in the past ten days, with the men who are defending her marching through her streets.

On that day, no more than on the Fourth, did any of the things the pessimists prophesied come true. The *Grosse Bertha* did not get to work. The night was quiet, — no air raid.

I stayed over until the morning of the sixteenth. I had to. I had a few necessary errands to do. I arrived in Paris on Saturday after many shops — now having what they called "*la semaine anglaise*" — were closed, and Monday, the day after the Fourteenth, was a holiday.

On Monday — the fifteenth — just before two o'clock, "bang" went the Big Bertha again, after a silence of three weeks. The first shot went harmlessly into the Seine, just missing a great mark, and after a lapse of about three hours it began again and put in several shells before dark. No one had any doubt that this presaged the new offensive, and we impatiently awaited the papers the next morning, which announced simply the fact that the Germans had attacked again on the front from Soissons, which they still hold, to Reims, which, although they have destroyed it, they have not been able to take since they were driven out in the battle of the Marne — that is to say, the nearest point to us.

Needless to tell you that I could not get back home quickly enough, although the little news we got seemed to be good. The Allies were holding them. This time the Germans had not been able to take Foch's army by surprise, as they had done in March and May. The attack, in extent, vigour and material seemed to be quite as formidable as that of March for Amiens.

Amélie met me at the station, and almost before I was out of the train she told me that the Americans had gone. The rest of the division, as I had foreseen, never came at all, and a *camion* came for those stranded on our hill, and carried them away.

She announced that the movement on our roads had been terrible for over forty-eight hours. The little road passing my gate had seen three hundred *camions* dashing by towards the canal on the day before, — the day the battle began. No sleep had been possible for two nights. She had had great difficulty in getting to the station, as the *route Nationale* was closed to all civilians. She had come down by the cart-track across the fields.

I lost some time at the station — my baggage had not come. It was not personal baggage — that is still waiting in Paris, to go to Versailles, if I have to. It was only a sack of sugar—oh, so precious!—and a case of condensed milk from an American rescue work, for the little refugee children and the old people. I had checked it the day before to save time. The station is always so crowded at train-time, and one has to wait so interminably to be weighed that I took advantage of the holiday, when I had nothing to do, to get it off. Incidentally, I am distressed about it, as it has not turned up yet, and that is six days ago. But on the day I returned I was too occupied with other anxieties to worry. Besides, it would have been a heavy load for Ninette to drag up the hill.

When we turned out from the station and crossed the Morin, the road looked clear, and after the guard had examined my papers—they seem to put a new guard every day, so it always has to be done—Amélie foolishly decided to try going up the *grande route*. We had not gone ten steps when a soldier with a red flag appeared in front of us, and turned us back, and we had to come up the *ruelle*. It is a very steep, very rough path, deeply rutted by farm-wagons and mowing-machines. The day was very hot. Ninette struggled along until I finally decided that, even in the blazing sun, I could climb on foot easier than I could sit behind her, and watch her strain and tug, so Amélie and I both got out and walked up, and I took in the news at the various stations we made to rest. The Americans had come to say good bye. They had said a lot of things, and she was sad because she had not understood a word. Meaux had been bombarded Monday and rather seriously damaged. Otherwise everything was as usual.

During the next two days the news was not bad, and then on Saturday came word that Foch had launched his counter-attack, and that it looked brilliantly successful. By Sunday morning we knew that the Germans had recrossed the Marne at Dormans, just south-east of Château-Thierry, hotly pursued by the Americans, — not a live German, unless he was prisoner, left on the south bank of the river. Every day since then the Germans have retreated. It is slow, but it is hopeful.

Ever since we have lived again on the map. Although we do not yet feel like calling it "a glorious victory" as you do, we do feel that never again will the Germans cross the Marne. If the Allies have been able to thrust them back now, when the Americans are not yet all ready, how can it be possible that we shall not hold them when we are getting stronger every day? We may be wrong, for one thing we do know, the Germans are still strong, and they will fight a terrible battle. They have still thirty unused divisions, and ever so much more artillery than we have, and a spy system that is amazing. They advanced from the Chemin des Dames in May to the Marne, thirty miles in six days. It has taken us nearly a week to push them back, mile by mile, a third of the way, so our relief is great, but our joy is cautious and well-contained.

I was speaking of the slowness of the retreat and the economy of it, so far as the Germans were concerned, this morning, to an officer, and he replied:

"It is better than we dared hope. If, before winter sets in, we can succeed in pushing them back to the strong positions in which they started in March, we shall feel more than satisfied, and hopeful, as by the spring the States will be really ready, and we shall be as strong as they are — at least — in artillery, and surely stronger in the air, and then we 'll finish them off, but it will still take time. They are mighty strong, and it is death we propose to deal out to them."

I imagine that this is a pretty fair statement of the situation. It makes me shiver sometimes to see how immediately hopeful you are. I have been that way myself, and I know what getting over it means.

Of course, a thousand things may happen — the *morale* may break in Germany. But those who know both the people and the country say it never will. So my present prayer is that the interim may be useful for the spreading of the conviction that this war *must* not stop when Germany is ready to make concessions, not even when she is ready to evacuate the lands she has seized, not even when she begins to whimper and regret — not until she is beaten to her knees, and not even then until she has been punished, and punished so severely that she cannot recover quickly, and left with a mark on her which she cannot conceal, not even by her most clever *camouflage*. She is a criminal nation. At large she is a danger to every nation and to every people on the face of the earth.

Now don't, I entreat you, reply that you have heard me preach prison reform. I have. I don't, of course, believe in treating even criminals like wild beasts — yet I don't know. At least I do believe in a restraint which protects the community. I never did, nor could, advocate pardon and liberty for jail-birds of marked criminal tendencies. The stigmata of crime are very persistent, and Germany bears the mark. Why should one cherish illusions for a race which one dares not harbour for the individual?

In an age which proudly calls itself civilized — whatever that may mean — Germany has waged a war such as even barbarous times never knew. It has not been a war of legitimate slaughter, which would have been terrible enough in a world of to-day's aspirations and pretension. It has been a war of violating women, abusing children, murdering inoffensive civilians, a war of rapine and wilful destruction, of breaking every law of the God whom they arrogantly claim, of every law man has made for the safeguarding of the community, a war of lies and cunning, by a people who claim the whole world, and deliberately deny the right of even existence to every one not born German, who arrogate to themselves the right to sin, and deny the right to live to all other races.

We are told that before the offensive of March twenty-first was launched the disciplinary laws which have long governed armies were all suspended by order of the German Commander-in-chief, and that the sack of all France on the hoped-for line of march from St. Quentin to the sea, and from the Chemin des Dames to Paris, was promised the German soldiers as their reward for victory, and what really happened seems to bear out the truth of the abominable statement. From St. Quentin to the Somme, and from the Chemin des Dames to the Marne, as well as the time permitted, they accomplished the object. The amount of booty they carried off was tremendous, and if everything did not fall as loot to the army, they at least achieved a destruction as complete as possible.

Naturally I did not see this with my own

eyes, but I have it on the testimony of soldiers who have come back from the devastated country, and whose word I have no reason to doubt. They tore to bits tapestries which they had not time to destroy. They smashed mirrors. They made firewood of the furniture in the humbler houses which was not good enough to send to Germany. They smashed dishes. If they did not destroy crops which they could not carry off, or if they left a pin anywhere it was only because in neither of their great pushes did they achieve their objective, and in both they met a resistance more tenacious than they expected, and which cost them dear, so that in certain places they were unable to accomplish under bombardment a destruction as thorough as they planned or had the will to do.

It is on things like this on which our minds fasten — for the flesh is weak and shrinks from such suffering as all that entails on the individual. Yet that is not Germany's worst crime. She has attacked the fundamental virtues towards which the world has been marching for centuries, and for which it has fought and bled many times, — the rights of peoples to choose their own fates; the rights of the individual to freedom; the hopes that free peoples have cherished of seeing the world become honest, and she has tried to bend all the world to the slavery of force.

In that lies her greatest crime, and it is for that abominable crime that she has to suffer, and must suffer, unless the world is to be thrown back a thousand years.

After all it is ideas that make history, not facts. From the beginning Man has shed his blood for ideas and opinions. They make history. That has marked the passing of people, of habits and customs, but the ideas have persisted. From the beginning — or rather in the short span of which we know anything — man has always had to fight and bleed for his ideas. Perhaps he always will. Who knows? Considering how little the majority understand this it is wonderful how heroically they do it.

As an example of that: the other day I met a young American officer — a lieutenant from the South — and in course of the conversation he remarked that France could "never recover herself," and when I smiled and shook my head at him, he added with a great deal of feeling:

"But you have not been out there. You have no idea of the destruction. There is not one stone on another. It is terrible. When this war is over, and all the costs counted, you will see that France is finished."

I had the folly to remark that all that would soon arrange itself, and that I counted as unimportant in the great scheme the material destruction, and was only concerned in the spiritual side of it all. Of course he did not understand. Why should he? So I thought it not worth while to state that personally I had a deep regret for every stone thrown down and a deeper sorrow for every young life so bravely given. He looked at me as if I was crazy. I suppose he thought me a white-haired old crank. Is it not true of all of us who read our history straight — or as straight as our limited intelligences will let us — that, though the life of each generation is made enthralling by the personal struggle, by new ways of making money, new ways of spending it, new ways of living and new ways of dressing and eating and amusing ourselves, these are not the vital things. If they were, there would have been few wars, in spite of adventurers, camp-followers and free-lances.

It is no palliation of the offence that the war the Germans forced on the world, with a criminal intent, has made of the fighting nations of the defence a people who will be all the finer for the struggle. It does not lighten Germany's sin that the world will have a nobler future, and living itself be the more worth while, for the serried effort the Allies have made. It is nothing to Germany's credit that, in the shoulder-to-shoulder and heart-to-heart sacrifices, and the heroically borne great grief, old differences have been forgotten and a better understanding achieved, that out of her sin good will come. She has done her most devilish to prevent that. The nations fighting out there in front of us to-day—on that long line from the Swiss frontier to the North Sea, and with stiff lips and brave eyes offering their best beloved on the altars of right, justice and liberty—must not be merciful except to a repentant sinner. That Germany will never be. It is not possible to her Kultur. A whining, lying, hypocritical—in fact a *camouflé*—penitent she may be; more than that is and will be for generations impossible for a nation and people bred to believe that what a people has strength to do, it has the right to do. If after all the experience the Allies have had they can be tricked into extending pity to a beaten Germany, why then they have fought and bled in vain. I suppose there are good Germans. Well, God must pity them, but they must, for the time, suffer for the crimes of their race as innocent children suffer for the sins of their fathers, and for the same reason; so why should man be foolishly lenient when neither the Almighty nor nature is?

We thought Belgium's tragedy could not be capped until Servia's capped it, and I am inclined to believe that Germany's deliberate debauching of Russia and her conscious mutilation of the soul of a people is her worst crime, for it may have arrested for centuries the slow and hoped-for evolution of a nation and a race in which we all may have had too much faith, but which, now that chaos has been dealt out to it, may be long in recovering, because one sees nowhere in sight yet the national hero who might wave a magic wand of personal love and magnetic patriotism and still the waters the Huns have troubled. The Allies have a duty — to aid in conjuring that spirit, but it can never be done while there is a German foot on Russian soil.

You ask in one of your late letters if I have been reading Cheradame on the "Eastern Question." Of course I have. His arraignment of facts is appalling. I own that. But it seems rather a pity that, while his statistics have tended to terrorize an easily terrorized people, some one does not add a footnote to remind the world, not only that there is a spirit in this great war — it has a soul as well as facts — and that if the Allies have *seemed* to neglect the eastern to devote themselves to the western frontier it must not be forgotten that, with all the forces they have, they have barely been able to hold the Huns at bay there. Besides, the vital thing is to *defeat* Germany, and it is immaterial *where* that is done so that it is done, and it is far from done yet. When Germany is well licked, and only then, will it be possible to deal with the races concerned in what has for so long been known as the Eastern Question, which really dates back to the seventeenth century, when Austria started on her "eastern route," if it does not go far back of that to the fall of Constantinople and the entrance of the Turk into Europe. With this great massacre ended, with Germany weakened and punished, and the Turks driven out, the Eastern Question can be dealt with by other means than a sword; and I dare say it will be found that, delivered from Prussian intrigue, the victorious Allies, with the power and the will to do it, will meet with aid and not opposition from the people concerned. But just as long as Germany is left with power to interfere such dreams can never be realized. Imagine the mentality of a people who can be lulled to sleep with Kaiser Bill's "Peace Talk," who can even tolerate a leader who states that the Allies are responsible for the continuation of the war because they refuse to stop fighting to protect their homes and liberties by acknowledging themselves beaten, pay the expenses of a war forced on them, and leave in the hands of the spoiler his loot in lands, subject peoples, and material!

After all the Kaiser made a mistake when he thought he was a second Napoleon I. Do you know what he is like? He is a reincarnation of Nabuchodonosor. Do read Chapters V and VI of the book of Judith in the Apocrypha if you don't believe me. And the King of the Assyrians had his Hindenburg, only even in those days of barbarity it did not occur to Holofernes to *poison* the wells and sources he seized when he set out to reduce Jerusalem.

I suppose you will reply that this comes very ill from me, who have been saying that I was tired of talk, and only wanted acts — words after achievements. Only a fool never changes her mind. I can't be really a fool, I change mine so often.

I note also that you object to my saying "dirty Germans" so often. That is only because I am becoming so very American — it's an ill war that brings about no good — ahem! That's all right. You may laugh. Besides, I supposed that you had heard the song the Amex boys brought over with them — a song which lists off what a soldier may expect each day in the week — shrapnel one day, then gas, then "over the top," down to the hospital on Saturday, and a funeral on Sunday, and each day's prayer is "Oh, you dirty Germans, I wish the same on you." Ever since I heard it in Paris we have never spoken of the Huns except as "dirty Germans," and even Amélie can say it, and prefers it to "les sales Boches," — the usual French designation, and of which "dirty Germans" is a literal translation.

Speaking of songs, I am told that the

Marines went "over the top" at Château-Thierry singing, "I want to go home, I am too young to die," and with cigarettes in their mouths. I don't vouch for that now, but it was told me by one of them, a sergeant who led the third wave over — thirty men. There were only two left with him when the *mitrailleuse* they encountered was silenced. But I can believe it. You ought to hear what the French say of the Amex boys, especially of how they fight when an assault becomes a hand-to-hand. They say that even when their ammunition is out, and their guns shot out of their hands, they use feet as well as fists, and rush it, heads down, as if in a football tussle. They assert that with experience they are going to make great soldiers. That emphasizes the blow at the German military ideas, does n't it?

I imagine that they have already dealt out a flush of surprises to the Germans. We have seen a large number of the prisoners here whom the Americans took — some of them not looking more than fifteen or sixteen years old. A few of them know a word or two of French, and when questioned about the Americans they said: "*Méchants les Américains — méchants!*" Are n't they wonderful? Strange people who feel the right to do the things they have done, and then think a soldier who fights back impolitely is "*méchant.*"

While I am writing this Amélie and Père have gone to look at the big gang of prisoners who have built our new double bridge, which crosses both the canal and the Marne at Mareuil, and the new road which will connect the *route nationale* with that to Compiègne, well west of Meaux. I have n't seen it since it was begun, but they have been down several times and tell me it is very handsome.

XXX

Remembrance Day, 1918

WELL, we are entering on the fifth year of the war. We were pained in 1914 when Kitchener prophesied a three years' war, and very cross when an American financier declared that it might last seven. I rather imagine five will settle it, but I am not prophesying. It is a long road still to the frontier. But to-day, when all the world, except Central Europe, is joining England in her solemn service of prayer, and the Allied chiefs are exchanging cables of hope and confidence, I may as well do my bit, by sending you my message. I feel especially inspired to do it by the fact that your letter just received expresses some surprise at what you call my losing my nerve, in the first week in June. Did I? Do you know, I can't remember. But you must know that the situation here was *desperate* from March twenty-first up to Foch's counter-offensive on July eighteenth. When I say desperate I mean just that.

Speaking of that time, I never told you that my famous sack of sugar never got here. By one of those errors that happen often, but by good luck never happened to me before, the cases I sent out from Paris on the morning of the fifteenth — the day the fifth offensive was launched — did not get put off at Esbly, where our narrow-gauge line meets the main line, but went on to the end, which, as the Germans were across the Marne at that time at Dormans, was La Ferté-sous-Jouarre, the next station beyond Meaux, and only about eleven miles from here. That night the railway station was bombarded by the Germans and destroyed and the station-master killed. So my precious sugar was burned up. I mention the fact only as interesting, and because it may account for what you call my nervousness. I am perfectly sure that if ever I were condemned to die for a cause, the hours of waiting for the end would be — shall we say? — trying.

But all that is changed, and one forgets easily.

On Friday night, at eight o'clock, the Allies entered Soissons again, and the pillar of the German position for the march on Paris by the valley of the Oise is lost to them. With both the valley of the Marne and that of the Oise closed to the invader, Paris is again safe, and we are again calm, and draw a long breath of relief, even though we know that we must count it lucky if, before winter, we can see the Huns back on the famous Siegfried line, from which they bounded last March, and to which they retreated in March of 1917. There they will be in almost impregnable positions, behind a long line of veritable fortresses, and in much better winter quarters than the Allies.

One of the prettiest things about this slow push forward, which *is* a victory, slow as it is, is the fact that every nation in arms for the Allied cause has taken part in it, and distinguished itself.

Our boys, fresh and untried, have more than held their own. I had a letter yesterday from a Californian who is with the Foreign Legion, who writes: "Since I saw you we have been through two campaigns with our beloved division. The first gave us all the sensations of the agony of retreat, the second all the exhilaration of a victory. And more than that, we have had the thrill of seeing our American troops fight side by side with the hardened *légionnaires* and *make good.*"

One more consoling thing. I have often asked myself, since I saw another war winter looming in sight, how our boys were going to stand the rough billets to which the *poilus* are accustomed,—so different from the camp quarters of their months of training at home, in England and even here. An American officer, who was here yesterday, tells me that, although the fighting regiments between the Marne and Fisme, which the boys from the States retook by assault, are *cantonned* in an absolutely destroyed country, under the roughest conditions, they take it gaily,—he has never heard the very smallest complaining.

So here we are at the beginning of the Year V.

We know that Germany is still strong. We cannot close our eyes to the knowledge that her death-struggle will be full of fearfulness. Still, with the days shortening—I had to light up last night at half-past seven in the salon, the first time I have had a light except in my bedroom since the last of May, which means winter will be here before we know it—we are really gayer than at the opening of any winter since the war began. It is not wholly because we are hardened to it. It is because the dawn of the new era begins to glow on the horizon of the future. We are moving slowly towards new days, for the world that was has gone, and the special colour of the days before the war can never be again. My Remembrance Day prayer is that the spirit moving over the fighting-line to-day and flinging its wide wings over the heads and hearts of all of us behind the lines may persist and make the nations as fine in the great after-the-war work ahead of them, as they have been noble, sacrificing, loyal to one another, and patriotic to their own flags in the great fight.

Printed in the United States
136649LV00006B/70/A

9 781437 3055